THE BEAN PIE

THE BEAN PIE

A REMEMBERING OF OUR FAMILY'S
FAITH, FORTITUDE, AND FORGIVENESS

TIFFANY GREEN-ABDULLAH, M.ED.

NEW DEGREE PRESS

COPYRIGHT © 2021 TIFFANY GREEN-ABDULLAH, M.ED.

THE BEAN PIE

A Remembering of Our Family's Faith, Fortitude, and Forgiveness

LCCN   2021925819

ISBN   978-1-63730-839-4   *Paperback*
            978-1-63730-904-9   *Kindle Ebook*
            978-1-63730-948-3   *Ebook*

To my mother, Shirley Green Wallace. Thank you for opening your heart and exposing me to your hidden pain. I hope this book provides you with understanding, peace, and forgiveness.

Contents

———

The Sankofa bird reminds us to reach back and gather the best of what our past must teach us so we can achieve our full potential as we move forward. Whatever we have lost, forgotten, foregone, or been stripped of can be reclaimed, renewed, preserved, and perpetuated.

Author's Note

———

I began authoring this book in the spring of 2020, shortly after the United States went into quarantine due to the COVID-19 virus. We were in quarantine for a little over a month. By we, I mean the entire country and most industrialized nations across planet Earth. I only went out three times to the grocery store and appointments between March and June 2020. Thankfully, the work and planning my husband, Tariq, and I put into Tarchitects, our architecture firm in 2019, kept us with projects to keep us going through 2020. Tariq continued leaving the house every day to check on construction sites and bid on new projects. He has always been "a closer," meaning he was able to get the deal successfully. I am grateful for his strength and calm. I am not always as calm.

My emotions were up and down during quarantine, but the shift in my lifestyle and the added time with my son and husband continue to be the best blessing out of all of this. Our life pre-quarantine was crazy busy every day, with a forty-minute drive to get our son to school on time. Then the hectic day continued working at either Georgia State University or Tarchitects. Both offices were within walking distance from one another in downtown Atlanta. Our home in a suburb outside Atlanta has great access to nature and trails, so the quarantine and the continued physical distancing became a time for reconnecting with one another and developing a plan to make it through the pandemic. As a family, we started the quarantine by taking early morning walks with our dog. At that time of day, there are very few people in the park.

Officials at our son's school canceled classes beginning March 16, 2020, when our son was nine years old. We decided to home school for the next school year and focus on his life skills and academics, including Islamic studies, music, architecture, math, and writing. Schools that met in person were shut down due to outbreaks of COVID-19 in 2020. When schools opened in person in 2021, children began to contract COVID-19, so we felt we were making the best decision to continue with homeschooling. I saw our little boy mature so much between spring 2020 through 2021. I would have missed so much of his development if our life had continued the same day-to-day schedule. He went through periods of loneliness, yet he became more initiative-taking, teaching himself animation, guitar, and the keyboard that came in 2021 for Eid (Islamic holiday gift). We did a virtual tenth birthday with a drive-by parade with gift bags and games on Zoom; his former schoolmate whose family moved back to Japan even joined the Zoom before he went to school, as it was a Monday in Japan. We focused on making the best of the time we were living in. He used technology to communicate with his friends consistently. By the summer of 2021, we, along with the families in our circle, became more comfortable with in-person play dates again. Unfortunately, the Delta variant made us recoil into physical distancing in the fall of 2021. I continue to worry about the long-term impact of this pandemic on his development.

It has been hard to know what to do or whose information to trust with this pandemic. I did not trust the news, given the history of mistreatment the Black community has faced about medical research—such as Henrietta Lacks.

Henrietta Lacks was a poor young mother in Baltimore, Maryland, who in 1951 visited the John Hopkins Hospital complaining of vaginal bleeding. Doctors discover she had cervical cancer. Her doctors sent a sample of her cancer cells to a tissue lab where the cells doubled every twenty-four hours, where most cells died in the lab. They named them "HeLa" cells from her first and last name. These HeLa cells have been used to assess the effects of radiation and poisons, study the human genome, learn more about how viruses work, and played a crucial role in developing the polio vaccine. All these things we great, but there was one caveat—Miss Lacks never consented to her cells being bought and sold millions of times. Her family did not know her cells were still living and were benefiting medical research until about 2000. On October 4, 2021, the *Washington Post* wrote, exactly seventy years after her death, Henrietta's descendants filed a lawsuit against a pharmaceutical company profiting thirty-five billion annually from her cells. "We want the world to know we want our family's legacy back." (*Washington Post*, 10/4/21)

I am doing everything I can as a mother and wife to keep us healthy and strong. We take vitamins, probiotics, cook at home with healthy foods, and clean and disinfect the surfaces. After a few weeks in quarantine, the walks reduced as our family business picked up. This was excellent for us because the economic gains in the country from the last ten years were lost in six weeks due to the pandemic.

As this "new environment" unfolds each day, this book becomes more important for me to write. All my life, I have had a close relationship with God. I started writing this book in a state of grieving. The life I was living prior to the coronavirus is over, and I believe life will not and should not go back to what it was before. I am an empath, so reading and hearing about thousands of people dying each day had me emotional, to say the least. I had to reduce my exposure to the media just to function. The only news source I watched consistently was Roland Martin Unfiltered. He provides an essential service to African Americans by providing news and African American experts we need for information relevant to our community and culture. One of Roland's weekly panelists is Dr. Greg Carr, the Chair of Afro-American Studies at Howard University. On Saturdays in May 2020, I started participating in Karen Hunter's "In Class with Carr" on YouTube. This course inspired me to continue researching for this book. It empowered me to cocreate a leadership network for African American Muslim women called Era of Woman as a response to George Floyd calling for his mother.

I have been a praying person ever since I was a little child. Hearing about death every day is overwhelming like a tsunami of sadness, especially now as the number of deaths rises. The medical and media sources like Roland Martin have verified the large numbers of death are increasingly Black people, like 70 percent Black in Chicago, my hometown. The *New*

York Times named Cook County Jail the biggest coronavirus hot spot in the nation as of April 7, 2020. Similar occurrences are taking place in New York, Louisiana, Georgia, and Detroit, having outlier numbers of Black people dying from coronavirus. That realization is a living nightmare.

There are so many things I still have not done. There are so many places I still have not seen. When things open back up, I intend to see the world. I want to visit Africa, including Senegal, Sierra Leone, and Guinea Bissau. I did an African Ancestry DNA test in spring 2021, and these are the places of my maternal ancestry. I also want to visit Egypt and Kenya. I especially want to make Hajj as a family. I want to take my oldest niece, Melony, to Paris, France, to fulfill my promise to her for her twenty-first birthday. She turned twenty-one in December 2020. I want to make a movie. I want to act in a movie. I want to have my wedding. Tariq and I got married at a small mosque in 2009 and then at city hall in 2011.

Our son is growing up in a world that is coming unglued. I want him to be healthy physically and emotionally and be a righteous man like his father. I want to see Tariq and I make a success of The Community Academy for Architecture and Design (TCAAD.org), the charter school we cofounded and were supposed to open in fall 2020. We pivoted to a virtual program in spring 2021. TCAAD is a long-term goal for our family.

Even with all these challenges, life continues, and we have to celebrate when we can. We celebrated Tariq's forty-second birthday and our eleventh anniversary during the quarantine. We kept it simple with a good home-cooked meal and a movie night with Muhammad. I am praying for a better future, but only Allah/God knows what will be. If my life does end because of this virus or any other reason, I have lived a great life, and I appreciate anyone willing to read about it in this book.

And where does the bean pie fit in?

It was 1967, and my Momma Shirley—only fourteen at the time—sat on my great-great-Aunt Daisy's mint green front porch on 71st Street in Chicago eating a piece of bean pie. Momma watched as Aunt Daisy and her husband, Uncle Ten, came out of Shabazz Restaurant, which was directly across the street.

Aunt Daisy told Momma Brother Robert, the manager, was looking for a new waitress now that Belinda intended to marry Muhammad Ali. Aunt Daisy had essentially settled things and gotten my mother the job, but to start working, Aunt Daisy had to tell Brother Robert she was sixteen. They walked over to the restaurant and made introductions as Brother Robert explained the responsibilities of the job. Thus began my mother's relationship with Shabazz Restaurant. She worked there until she was nineteen.

Soon after Momma began working at Shabazz, she was on her lunch break eating Aunt Daisy's bean pie again. Bean pie is made of navy beans, spices, butter, sugar, and vanilla, so it is more than a dessert. It could be breakfast, lunch, or a dessert. Brother Robert asked young Shirley if she would ask Aunt Daisy to share the bean pie recipe with him. Shirley walked across the street and made the request to Aunt Daisy. She wrote down the recipe, and my mother carried it back over to Brother Robert. Soon after, the restaurant was making the pies. The Nation of Islam, which owned the restaurant since the 1930s, only began selling bean pies in 1970. (*Muhammad Speaks*, 1971.) In the 1960s, Black people could not eat just anywhere. This restaurant was also where Black people on the south side of Chicago ate, including musicians like the Temptations, movie stars, athletes like Muhammad Ali, leaders like Farrakhan, and other notables.

In conversations over the years with my mother, I would always ask: Why did Aunt Daisy just give over the recipe and not get any of the financial gains? Momma said the request from Brother Robert was not really a request. If she had not given up the recipe, she could have been admonished by the Nation. As Dr. Ula Yvette Taylor wrote in *The Promise of Patriarchy* (2017), the Nation of Islam "promised responsible patriarchs for the betterment of the nuclear family and, ultimately, the larger Black Nation" (6). That was a packed statement, and it has taken many years of research to learn what I have discovered thus far. There continue to be nuances to all the stories, including the unknown history of the bean pie, the relationship between Aunt Daisy, Elijah Muhammad and the Nation of Islam, my grandmother's story, and determining who was my biological grandfather.

The bean pie is an American icon today. The food and culture of African Americans is a direct link to the American culture as well as African. There are many similarities between our "soul food" and common African staples. Our greens are likening to Ethiopian gomet or Nigerian efo riro. Nigerian fufu is like corn bread. The precursor of the bean pie was the Nigerian Moi-Moi, a versatile bean dish. We brought our cooking and traditions through enslavement and remnants of our faith that we remixed through a fascination with Orientalism and entertainment to create the religious systems we practice in the US and abroad. As we reverted to Islam in the 1930s, the honorable Elijah Muhammad warned the community some of those staple foods were not good for our health—including pork and white flour. This rebellion against common place food changed the culinary history of America. One of the outshoots of this culinary education for Black Muslims is the bean pie. If you search the internet for the history of the bean pie, you will find general explanations such as:

The pie dates to the 1930s, when the founder of the Nation of Islam, Elijah Muhammad, told his followers to eschew pork and unhealthy starches like cornbread and adhere to a healthful diet, with a particular focus on the navy bean. Muslims created the bean pie in part as a healthier substitute for the sweet potato pie. (Seattle Times, June 19, 2011)

I have been curious about the origin story of the bean pie since 2009, when I converted to Islam. Unfortunately, her history is limited and hidden in family histories we are losing as the elder Black Muslims transition. Depending on where one lives and one's proximity to a Black Muslim mosque is usually the easiest place to buy a bean pie. Outside of those narrow geographies, one would be hard-pressed to eat a bean pie unless you made it yourself, which is what I began to do to recover my family's heritage.

Every Ramadan after 2010, I would make bean pies, and the idea of developing a bean pie business became clearer as the orders rolled in. Was the oral tradition of my family an exaggeration? What is the real story? Was there any way of knowing? I had to regroup over the last few years and kept asking questions, interviewing elders, and scouring every book I could find on the Nation of Islam. I consistently found very little to no information on the bean pie.

Aunt Daisy was in Detroit in the 1930s per oral history when the Nation of Islam started. Aunt Daisy moved to Chicago in the mid-1930s. Aunt Daisy and her sister, Ceola, raised my grandmother in Chicago, where she was born in 1933. Aunt Daisy was a close confidante of Elijah Muhammad and was often at his home for dinner. Daisy is mentioned in the book, *The Promise of Patriarchy*, placing her in Chicago in 1941. I heard the stories passed down about the white carpet he had throughout his home. There is a lack of documentation about Black women's roles in history generally. This is one of the reasons for this book.

Black families have histories, significant histories, often lost from one generation to the next because we have had to leave places for economic gain or to escape brutality. Those histories uncover pain and secrets elders want to forget, not knowing there is a consequence for future generations not having a sense of how they arrived. This book is a mix of biography refracted from oral history, genealogy research, research about the time periods, geographic locations, culture, interviews with my mother, Shirley, about her life, and everything she could tell me about my great-great-Aunt Daisy and Grandma Shirley. It is also autobiographical, sharing my experiences and commentary that bring this story into the present day.

This lack of history leaves a hole in the mental state of our offspring. This book will explore the stories of our family's past to make up for all the stories left half told. Initially, this book was only going to be about the bean pie and how Aunt Daisy created it. As I began to ask about my mother's past, I saw the bean pie as my connector to the history of multiple generations of women: my mother, Shirley; Grandmother Shirley; great-great-Aunt Daisy; great-Grandmother Bessie; second-great-Grandmother Ceola; third-great-Grandmother Mattie; and fourth-great-Grandmother Caroline "Carrie."

It is important to me to write about the lost story of Aunt Daisy and how she moved from Opelika, Alabama, to Chicago, Illinois, and how she was one of the earliest members of the Nation of Islam. I wanted to write about my grandma and what happened before the birth of my Uncle Sweetie and mother when she was between the ages of seventeen to nineteen. Was Wilbur Green, Sr. my actual grandfather? Why did my grandma treat my momma differently than her other five children from Jessie "Sonny" Boyd? Did anyone know the abuse she endured by his hand? Or that she likely suffered from postpartum depression after having baby after baby for nearly seven years? Why was she mean sometimes, and can we break that cycle? Why did Aunt Daisy give special treatment to momma and Uncle Sweetie? I had my mother do a genetic test and discovered new family information that helped explain some issues of my grandmother's upbringing but also created more questions. My grandma lost her mother at three years old. I researched the trauma of bereaved children. I initially did not understand the ramifications of that loss and how it changed her entire life.

This book is a tribute to all these incredibly strong women in my family. They endured pain beyond comprehension so our family can exist today. My role is to tell their stories so we can uplift and honor them, understand the impact of their trauma, and transform it into a hopeful future and work on forgiving them and ourselves. I want my children and future generations to know they are not here by accident. The toil of our ancestors, including their successes and mistakes, make us who we are. No one is perfect, but it takes strength to keep going and learn from one generation to the next. I am leaning on that strength as I write this book during one of the most challenging times the world has seen.

This is also a cautionary tale for families to document their history so as not to find themselves in a similar position as me, having to fill in the gaps from oral histories and memories, especially for deceased relatives. I have always been a reader of history, especially about successful people and successful families. I have learned most of us are not free from hardship and struggle. It is how I have dealt with the effects of the trauma that has determined my success in life. Above all, the four central characters I will write about have overcome oppression, poverty, addiction, abuse, neglect, and grief to make it from Alabama to Detroit and then Chicago, Nashville, and Atlanta. I hope this begins a tradition of family storytelling to move us forward while never forgetting to look backward. *Our power is in our story and how we got here.* The bean pie made me look back and, like the Sankofa bird, gather the best of what our past could teach me so we can achieve our full potential as we move forward. I asked questions about it and about Aunt Daisy, which led me to seek a better understanding of my grandmother and my mother. These are the women who raised me, so knowing them better would help me to know myself better and hopefully help the rest of the family know themselves better. The oral traditions were strong, and as I became a Muslim, I learned there were major holes in the history of the bean pie. Perhaps my family was standing right in the center of it all.

PART 1

REMEMBERING THE BEAN PIE

CHAPTER 1

Young Daisy

FALL 1910

The sun hadn't come up yet, but Daisy was already awake. She was lying between her two sisters, Ceola, age ten, and little Mattie, who was snoring well beyond her three years. They could hear the trains rumbling in the still of the morning from five miles away. She enjoyed the solitude of those moments before everyone would be bustling to work on the farm. Ceola rolled over and whispered, "Go wake Momma."

Their father, John Kennon, died shortly after little Mattie was born. She didn't remember much about him. He was gone a lot when they lived in Tuscaloosa, Alabama. Momma Mattie brought them all back to Opelika, Alabama, to live with her family after he died.

Daisy was eight years old, and her job was to help her momma prepare breakfast and lunch for her Uncle William, whom they lived with. That morning she boiled the meal with molasses. There was some leftover salt pork, which she placed on a plate over the steaming pot to warm it up. She wrapped the salt pork and cornbread in a piece of paper and his meal in a small pot. She poured a cup of coffee in a mug and sat it all out at the corner of the table so he could grab it on his way out the door.

William was the oldest male. He handled the farm, so he had to be there before first light to feed the mule. The mule was in for another hard day of work tilling the land. Daisy then helped her mother serve the meal and a small piece of cornbread for all of them. Ceola got up and washed and dressed little Mattie. She fed her and took her down the road to Aunt Sarah and Uncle Brandton, twelve-year-old twins who managed the little children for the family and neighbors.

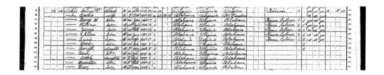

1900 Census showing the Scaife family without Mattie.

1910 Census showing the Scaife family without Grandpa George.

In 1910, the entire Scaife family lived at Grahams Store Farm in Lee County, Opelika, Alabama. Lee County is home to Auburn University and is an industrious area due to the creeks and waterways. Some believe Grandma and Grandpa were enslaved on the land and stayed after slavery, but no one has confirmed that information.

Grandpa George died sometime between 1901–1909. Grandma Caroline "Carrie," out of concern for the safety of her family, did not want them to go too far from the farm due to the brutality of White people in the community. Sometimes, as the uncles came of age, they would go off and work outside of the county but often returned with a wife. They were still sharecropping as a family. Daisy's mother, Mattie, was the oldest at twenty-nine and managed the younger Scaifes in the fields. Aunt Dorah was sixteen and very close to Daisy. Uncle Kanty was fifteen, and Uncle William was twenty-five.

Daisy filled her days helping and learning from Grandma Carrie on how to cook and sew. Uncle Perry was ten, the same as Ceola, so they worked in Grandma Carrie's garden for the family's day-to-day food. Ceola tended the garden of beets, black eye peas, greens, green peas, strawberries, onions, sweet potatoes, corn, collard, turnip and mustard greens, tomatoes, cabbage, okra, peanuts, and different herbs. Grandma Carrie was smart about home remedies and taking care of anyone with teas and tonics she made in her kitchen from foods from her garden. Uncle Perry took care of the chicken coop and removed the eggs used for baking bread and cakes.

All the children would work with Grandma Carrie to can everything when it came out of the ground. This was the way they preserved food to last outside of the harvest times. As they worked, Grandma Carrie passed down stories through her cooking.

TIFFANY GREEN-ABDULLAH Family Tree

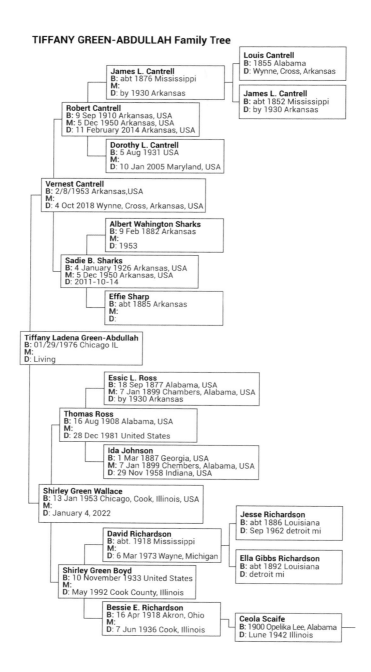

James L. Cantrell
B: abt 1876 Mississippi
M:
D: by 1930 Arkansas

Louis Cantrell
B: 1855 Alabama
D: Wynne, Cross, Arkansas

James L. Cantrell
B: abt 1852 Mississippi
D: by 1930 Arkansas

Robert Cantrell
B: 9 Sep 1910 Arkansas, USA
M: 5 Dec 1950 Arkansas, USA
D: 11 February 2014 Arkansas, USA

Dorothy L. Cantrell
B: 5 Aug 1931 USA
M:
D: 10 Jan 2005 Maryland, USA

Vernest Cantrell
B: 2/8/1953 Arkansas,USA
M:
D: 4 Oct 2018 Wynne, Cross, Arkansas, USA

Albert Wahington Sharks
B: 9 Feb 1882 Arkansas
M:
D: 1953

Sadie B. Sharks
B: 4 January 1926 Arkansas, USA
M: 5 Dec 1950 Arkansas, USA
D: 2011-10-14

Effie Sharp
B: abt 1885 Arkansas
M:
D:

Tiffany Ladena Green-Abdullah
B: 01/29/1976 Chicago IL
M:
D: Living

Essic L. Ross
B: 18 Sep 1877 Alabama, USA
M: 7 Jan 1899 Chambers, Alabama, USA
D: by 1930 Arkansas

Thomas Ross
B: 16 Aug 1908 Alabama, USA
M:
D: 28 Dec 1981 United States

Ida Johnson
B: 1 Mar 1887 Georgia, USA
M: 7 Jan 1899 Chembers, Alabama, USA
D: 29 Nov 1958 Indiana, USA

Shirley Green Wallace
B: 13 Jan 1953 Chicago, Cook, Illinois, USA
M:
D: January 4, 2022

David Richardson
B: abt. 1918 Mississippi
M:
D: 6 Mar 1973 Wayne, Michigan

Jesse Richardson
B: abt 1886 Louisiana
D: Sep 1962 detroit mi

Ella Gibbs Richardson
B: abt 1892 Louisiana
D: detroit mi

Shirley Green Boyd
B: 10 November 1933 United States
M:
D: May 1992 Cook County, Illinois

Bessie E. Richardson
B: 16 Apr 1918 Akron, Ohio
M:
D: 7 Jun 1936 Cook, Illinois

Ceola Scaife
B: 1900 Opelika Lee, Alabama
D: Lune 1942 Illinois

"We ate what we grew and whatever we had. My momma would make food, wear her clothes, wrap her hair, and praise God in the ways her momma taught her. We have been here a hundred years since they took my momma's momma from Africa. My grandma made my momma remember words so she would not forget where she came from. One word I remember was her tribe's name, 'Mandinka.' I can't read and write, but I can cook the food the way she taught me and her momma taught her. So, I want you all to remember we go back before slavery and before America. I am going to teach you to cook things like you were there, even though we never stepped a foot off this land. I want you to remember," Grandma expressed in a tone of expectation.

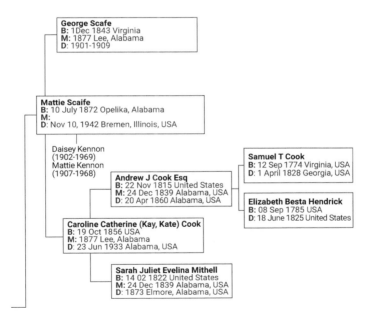

Tiffany's family tree. This book focuses on her maternal side.

"What was your favorite thing, your momma cooked?" asked Daisy.

Grandma closed her eyes and cupped her right hand with her left hand over it in a rolling motion. "My momma would mash beans up and season them with fish, eggs, or pork and roll them into a ball and put them into a leaf then boil them. That was my favorite."

"What was that called?" asked Ceola.

"She would call it mo-mo," said Grandma.

Daisy asked, "What else do you remember?"

"I remember how when my momma was happy or sad or just needed to figure something out, she would walk in a circle and sing and stump her feet in a rhythm. But on Sundays, the only day the enslaved people got to rest, they would meet in a wood house at the edge of the plantation, and it had no windows. Everyone would walk in a circle and say prayers out loud, and everyone else would respond. As they walked, they stumped, and the boards of the floor would jump. They called this the 'ring shout.'" Grandma smiled in her recollection.

"That's like at church how the pastor calls out to the Lord, and the church people start talking back and singing and clapping, and the organ man makes everyone get out their seat from the rhythm of his playing," said Brandton.

"Yes, darling, that's where it started," chimed Grandma.

"I am going to make food like you, Grandma," Daisy proudly proclaimed.

Daisy couldn't read or write at that time, but she was helpful, considerate, and insightful. She paid attention to everything and everyone around her. She learned in a large family to be seen but not heard. She loved to run errands for Grandma Carrie with her aunties and uncles in town. They would take the horse and wagon to buy fabric, seeds, and tools for the farm. In the spring and fall, they would set up a stand and sell canned goods.

The winter of 1909 through summer 1910 was especially brutal across Alabama, with over a dozen Black men lynched by mobs. Everyone stayed close to the farm, but it was nearing time to sell the canned goods, get winter supplies, and connect with the strong Black community in Montgomery. Montgomery had become a seat of power for Black Alabama since the end of slavery because they received the right to vote, but it was overturned in 1901 (Smith, 2021). The Black community was still strong in commerce due to their proximity along the Alabama River.

Momma Mattie, Aunt Dorah, Ceola, and Daisy traveled to Montgomery with Uncle William. Grandma preferred the rest of the men stay on the farm. It was a four-hour ride to Montgomery. They left early in the morning so they could arrive right before the sun came up. After they set up their stand on the Black side of Main Street, Aunt Dorah asked if she could go buy fabrics with Daisy. Mattie gave Dorah $1.50 for notions and at least ten yards of different cottons.

Uncle William said, "Okay now, stay safe and come right back."

Daisy and Dorah walked a quarter mile to the White part of Main Street to the fabric store. They went through the back door, as was typical during segregation. They stood and waited until the shop lady asked what they wanted. Dorah spoke mildly, "I need ten yards of fabric and notions, ma'am." The shop lady waved them over to that section of the store. Daisy looked quickly through the section and pointed to three different colors (yellow, blue, and brown) that could work for new dresses for the girls and a few pants for the men. They moved quietly and quickly. As the shop lady began cutting their fabric, they heard a loud commotion outside.

The store windows went dark as a crowd of White men filled the street, shouting as they walked past the fabric store toward the jail down the street. Dorah grabbed Daisy's hand, and the clerk finished the cutting, shoved it toward Dorah, and told them to hurry back home. They had to walk the same way the men were walking to get to the Black part of Main Street, where the jail was conveniently located. They waited outside the back of the store until the men walked to the front of the jail.

"Let us have them!" the men screamed.

They were talking about two men the jail was holding before their trial who had assaulted a young girl. Dorah and Daisy hung to the wall and tried to be invisible as they made their way near the men. The men quieted when the sheriff came onto the jail steps.

The sheriff with a badge proudly displayed on his shirt yelled at the men with a menacing smirk, "Go on now, let us do our job. Those men will be tried and convicted. Don't you worry."

There was a roar through the mob. The men yelled back, "Let us have them now!"

"That's not going to happen," the sheriff replied.

Daisy and Dorah made it past the back of the men and were on the other side when the crowd started moving toward the Black side of Main Street again. Momma was watching out for the girls and started running toward them when they tiptoed past the men. William had already packed up the wagon when the girls ran into Momma's arms. She hugged them tight and pushed them onto the wagon.

The mob stopped at the cab stand when they saw a Black man sitting in the front seat of his taxi. The man looked frightened and nervously shouted, "I am waiting for my passenger to take her back home."

The men did not care. They were out for blood. They snatched John Dell out of the taxi and held him in the air over the crowd (Memorial in Alabama Will Honor Victims of Lynching, 2016). Uncle William stopped the wagon at the sight of this atrocity. The mob surrounded Mr. Dell and began senselessly attacking him.

Momma yelled at William, "Go now!"

They pulled out behind Main Street to escape the mob. After a minute or so, they heard gunshots and the mob cheering. They executed John Dell in the town square.

William did not stop on the way back to Opelika. No one spoke either. They never spoke of it to the family. That day etched itself into everyone's mind, but especially Daisy and Dorah, who had nightmares of the mob grabbing them.

Daisy and Dorah would not talk about that incident again until the 1940s when Dorah joined the Nation of Islam and moved to Chicago to be near Daisy.

FALL 1920

Daisy was eighteen and dreamed of the day when she would leave Alabama and go up North to a place where she could feel safe. The community was buzzing with the prospects that awaited in northern cities like Chicago and Detroit. There was a steady trickling of young people escaping to those cities due to the brutality of the police and Ku Klux Klan. White people continued their mob rule, not letting the justice system play out.

The lynching continued. There were 361 documented racial terror lynchings in Alabama, and five are known to have occurred in Lee County (Brown and Nichols, 2021). The bad light it brought on the town reduced the number of lynchings, but racism was always present. They had slowed between 1912–1917 due to the pressure of activists like Ida B. Wells, but lynchings began to increase again in the iteration of race riots during the "Red Summer," a time between 1917–1921

(Sieber, K., 2021). Black soldiers returning from World War I found the opposite of the freedom they experienced in Europe. The Great Migration North was creating tension over housing and territory redistribution within cities. Race riots brought unseen violence against prosperous communities built by self-determined economically successful Black families throughout the country. White jealousy led to the burning of towns such as Tulsa, Oklahoma, known as "Black Wall Street."

The threat of violence and the violence they saw concerned the family so much that many had already moved up North. Most of the family moved to Chicago, Illinois, and Akron, Ohio. The only people left in town were Grandma Carrie, Momma Mattie, Ceola, Auntie Dorah, Auntie Sarah, and Uncles Brandt and William. Grandma Carrie, now sixty-four, was being taken care of by Momma, and the rest of the family was sending money. The money they received from the uncles and aunties kept them in a decent status and allowed William to buy some land, so everyone was working it as well as other jobs. Daisy was even able to go to school and learn how to read and write.

Daisy's sewing skills continued to improve under the tutelage of Grandma Carrie. She used her advanced domestic and tailoring skills to make a living. As an early teen, Daisy washed clothes for White women, but as her skills for sewing and tailoring increased, she transitioned from washing to repairing and light tailoring. People did not throw away clothes the way some do today.

One of the women gave Daisy a pattern for a typical lady's hat from 1920. Daisy taught herself how to make the hat. She then tried to create the styles she saw from the ladies about town and those stopping through on their way to Atlanta or New Orleans. She could not make as much money as she wanted because Momma did not allow her to spend on flamboyant fabrics. Daisy would buy secondhand clothes and make hats for herself, her family, and her friends.

On Sundays, the family would all get dressed in their best and attend Bethesda Baptist Church. Bethesda was the first Black church in Opelika, and all the long-standing Black families attended.

Daisy loved putting on her finest on Sundays and meeting in the church basement after service to show off her dress and matching hat. Her favorite time was Sunday dinner at home when everyone came together, including friends and neighbors, over some fried chicken, greens, black eye peas, corn, cornbread, sweet potatoes, sweet potato pie, and lemonade.

She would sit quietly, learning about the world from the adults and friends who visited. All those conversations she listened to taught her lessons that would serve her well as she went out further into the world. Daisy learned to be cautious about how she dressed. She learned she didn't want to be too flashy in a town where White people didn't take kindly to Black people believing in themselves. White people always said it was Black people who were lazy and uneducated, but Daisy could not name a lazy person except a baby. What Daisy saw and learned from working with White people was the clear opposite. They always wanted everything done for them. She was frustrated about always having to take care of White people and play small around them, but she kept it inside. She designed her dresses simple yet well-made, but at night she would put on the fancier dresses in her closet and prance around the house. She believed she could find a way to a better life.

Some of the family would return to Opelika from Chicago and Akron for Bethesda Church revivals in August. The family visited a few times each year. Even with the violence in the South, keeping family ties was paramount. Grandma Carrie wanted her grandchildren and great-grandchildren around her for as long as she could to pass on her cooking, stories, and traditions. All the children would be shipped there in the summer to get them out of those hot cities. It was unbearable for the children living in apartments in the steamy summers. At least they could run around and get outside when they went south for the summer. It was a lot of fun growing up with all their cousins.

Opelika, Alabama, was an industrious city with an illustrious history. The White settlers moved 23,000 Creek people who originally controlled Alabama, so White people could control the waterways and control the main industry, textile making (Huffman, K. 2018). Over time, other big factories moved in. It was a rail connection between Atlanta and New Orleans, and one could get pretty much anything in town, such as textiles and different foods from other places in the South.

All those companies that built themselves up in Opelika did not allow Black workers to hold the main jobs. Black people could work at night to clean or cook in the canteens but not eat there. Daisy wanted to experience more of the city life and to gain work experience. Thanks to all those mornings in the kitchen with Momma and those days helping Grandma, she was a great cook.

Daisy started cooking for a factory lunchroom when she was sixteen. She learned to have one ear up like a beacon. One day, the owner brought some young men in for a tour and lunch.

"My cooks are amazing," bragged the owner.

Daisy served their plates and gave the young tourist an extra serving of her greens and cornbread. They took the plates without a word of thanks to Daisy.

The men ate their lunch and continued talking about business.

"I want to expand into other textiles used in cars since the automobile industry is expanding up North," said the owner.

The visitor replied, "That's a good idea. They need more textiles for the seats and floors. I can give you the address of some suppliers I know up there."

"I will get my secretary to send a post immediately," the owner said.

"You can make a ton, but make sure you can keep your production going. I see you do not employ negros on the floor. You might want to try something to keep them in town. I see the train yard packed every Friday from here to Atlanta with negros moving North."

The owner winced. "I don't know about that. My boys won't work with them, and then I would have to pay them a higher wage."

Daisy stayed close by, listening to their conversations, but acted like she was cleaning. She had a keen interest in any talk about money, deals, and opportunity up North. They never paid her any attention. They overlooked her as a Black girl. They could never imagine she would aspire to be in business one day. But she still learned industriousness by seeing and watching those around her. And she knew if she could just get somewhere where she could find an opportunity, she would take it. She could make it for herself.

The train came through Opelika to Atlanta, so for a time she thought about starting in Atlanta, but the brutality was no different there. Georgia was second only to Mississippi in lynching from 1877 to 1950, at 654 and 589 (Staff, AJC, 2017), and Alabama was number five at 361. She continued her planning and searching for a better possibility for her move.

Then the next summer of 1921, the First Lady of Bethesda asked her to cook for a sendoff party for young women and men heading out to Detroit. They were moving to get jobs in those new automobile factories. Detroit had a good feel to it. She wanted to go with them, but she was not ready financially, and neither was Momma, who felt torn up every time someone else left.

One of the girls going to Detroit was her best friend, Lula. They talked about going for years, but it surprised Daisy when she found out Lula was leaving this time. Daisy was setting up the food after church service.

Lula said, "Daisy, I want you to have my aunt's address where I will be staying. If you ever want to come up North, write to me so I can help you, okay?"

Daisy looked at Lula with a sad smile. "Maybe, one day." She did not want Lula to know how sad she was about her leaving. "Lula, I have something for you too," said Daisy, handing Lula a bag of special treats she made.

Daisy had also been making her own version of Grandma's "mo-mo" recipe. She made Lula a dozen of the bean balls with salted pork and a dozen with honey and spices so she had something sweet that could last the trip. Lula hugged Daisy hard, and they both wept.

Daisy said, "Okay, enough," and kept setting up, but all the while, she was doing calculations in her head.

I need $23 for a train ticket. I need money for room and board for at least six months in case I cannot find a job. I can always cook somewhere if I need money... She knew she needed to save more money, but she made a goal only within herself to leave Opelika the next spring and move to Detroit with Lula and be part of the Great Migration to the North.

Lula mentioned again, "Well, if you do ever come up, make sure it is in the early spring. It gets very cold, my aunt writes, so you're going to need time to get adjusted before the winter sets in."

Daisy nodded. She understood and added that to her mental plan.

Unfortunately, Daisy's plans were put on delay for a few years for different reasons. One was Momma just could not part with her. She needed her to help with Grandma. Ceola snuck off to Akron because she was tired of being in Opelika. Ceola was working on Momma to move there with Grandma. William was looking at going to Chicago, so everyone was really working on Momma. Daisy saved every dime she could cooking and even made simple hats the church ladies liked.

But finally, in 1925, at the age of twenty-three, she left Opelika from Birmingham on a train to Detroit. Her mother and family said their goodbyes at the house. They had seen too many families cut loose when their young people left for fear they would never see them again. They loaded her up with hoecakes, salt pork, dried figs, and jars of black eye pea salad. Daisy had her sweet "mo-mo" recipe. Uncle William and Uncle Brandton escorted her to the train station in Birmingham. She would miss them all.

"Girl, I'm going to miss your cooking. Now who's going to make my grits, right?" Uncle William said sadly and jokingly.

"You know Momma can cook your grits. She taught me." She also told him, "You know how to make it too, so don't go starving yourself being lazy."

He shook his head in submission to his young niece, whom he loved like a daughter. Daisy traveled with a group of eight other young people (three ladies and five men). They were dressed in their best when they left Alabama for their new life in Detroit.

CHAPTER 2

Daisy's Eatery

—

Daisy arrived in Detroit, Michigan, on a bright April morning in 1925. It was spring, but like none she could recall. It was cold. Her overcoat was not adequate. Her companions all huddled in the station, but shortly afterward, Lula arrived to pick her up. She would start this new life staying with Lula and her family.

The Black population of Detroit doubled to 80,000 between 1920 and 1925 when Daisy arrived (Bates, B. 2012). The city was restricting renting to Black people and creating all Black neighborhoods, mainly on the eastside of Detroit. With so many Black folks arriving every day from all points in the South to work in the automobile industry, in addition to racist practices of the police infiltrated by the Ku Klux Klan, Mattie did not want Daisy without support in Detroit. Lula worked in a factory and shared a two-bedroom apartment with her auntie and uncle. Momma Mattie only let Daisy go after corresponding with Lula's aunt. She really wanted her to go to Chicago, where her sister and brothers were. Daisy was quiet but stubborn. She knew what she heard and read in the newspapers (Bates, B, 2014). Detroit had more opportunity for now, but it was not without discord.

Lula got her a job in the factory not long after Daisy arrived. Daisy's job was to refill buckets with screws that had fallen to the floor. It was backbreaking work. The place was dirty and dusty. She worked there for a month out of courtesy, but within that month the inside of her hands became infected from blisters, and she could hardly get up each morning from her body aching from carrying those buckets of screws. Daisy was earning twenty-four cents per hour filling those buckets. She knew there had to be another way.

She thought about going into business for herself. She noticed everyone outside at lunch with wrapped sandwiches or looking for a place to eat. She began by making meals in their small kitchen when everyone left for work and selling them outside the factory during lunch. She sold the meals for $0.10 each. With a one-day trial investment of $1.20 for potatoes, sausages, onions, bread, and soda pop, she made $2.75. She knew she could make this work.

She only made $9.60 per week at the factory, and her body could not take the work. She quit the factory job and set out as a full-time entrepreneur. She switched up her menu to include a light breakfast of a biscuit, sausage, and egg sandwich she made the night before. She would go out in the morning and afternoon. She made $22.50 the second week. She also altered clothes for ladies and began making hats again. She knew bringing her sewing machine would pay off. This time, she could show flair because Detroit had a jumping nightlife, and Black people were serious about looking good and being seen.

In 1927, Daisy, Lula, her aunt and uncle, and another couple all moved into a larger rooming house on 2220 Gratiot Avenue. Daisy found the place through her network and negotiated with the owner to let them live there on both floors. The rent was $37 per month. Each couple paid $8, and Daisy paid $13. They pulled their resources, but Daisy had the larger share of the rent because she took over downstairs with access to Gratiot Avenue. It had a large kitchen and front room right at street level and a bedroom in the back for Daisy. She recalled her days working in the factory lunchroom. She believed in her ability to run a little restaurant after her mobile business made her a decent living.

Front (2007) and back (2020) of 2220 Gratiot where Aunt Daisy ran her eatery (Image courtesy of Google maps).

There were three rooms upstairs and a bathroom. The family needed those rooms since Lula was getting married. It was still a luxury for each couple to have their own room, and at the time none of them had children, so they maximized their time and resources in this new Detroit that was growing diverse, exciting, dangerous, crowded, and racist. Daisy bartered for four small tables and one larger one and purchased her first real bed with a headboard for $22.95. The building was within walking distance of shops, including the Eastern Market, where she could buy every type of food in the world. It was a brisk walk to the Detroit River and Belle Isle. The area was bustling and a place where she would cook and serve the people.

The neighborhood was very diverse. The Vermick family were Russian Jews, and Mr. Hing from China owned a building largely lived in by the Lamus family from Greece. There was a large Muslim population made up of Arabs, Turks, Syrians, and Mexicans. Daisy's customers were as diverse as the neighborhood, with the majority being Black. She would serve anyone who could be respectful, pay, eat quickly (breakfast and lunch were mainly to go in brown paper bags), and not be loud. There wasn't room for large parties. As time passed, she got to know people—even some who were very special to Detroit.

In 1927, Daisy opened at 6:00 a.m. for breakfast of grits, bacon, chicken sausage, eggs, coffee, and biscuits for $0.15. Lunch was $0.20, and dinner was $0.50 by reservation only. Lula and the other tenants helped her cook from 4:00 a.m. to 6:00 a.m. for part of their rent. The rest of the day, they worked at the plants. She hired other girls to help cook under her direction as needed and to serve. She also had two doormen on shifts.

"Daisy, I have everything prepared for the morning rush," Lula said as she also poured her and Daisy coffee at 4:45 a.m. The new girl walked into the kitchen.

"Miss Daisy, thank you for giving me a chance to learn from you. No one wants to hire a girl with so many men out of work, and I just could not take being a maid for White people any longer. I didn't know what I would get and what they would want to do to me," she admitted.

Daisy and Lula shook their heads. They knew well what she meant. Working as a maid could make you vulnerable to the brutality of the woman or the man of the house.

"You are fine, Dinah. The first thing is to make sure the coffee is on, which Lula did, but also prep the eggs and biscuit," Daisy said as she continued teaching her the ins and outs of the morning rush.

The day went quickly, and the eatery shut down at 2:00 p.m. so Daisy could rest and the girls could clean up and set the dining room up for dinner. Daisy only allowed ten for dinner each night, and her reservations were nearly full every night of the week for weeks in advance. Most people would put their names down on the list if there were any openings when they came by for breakfast or lunch. By 1929, her place was well known as an exclusive supper club at night. She attracted the who's who of Black Detroit. Her income was estimated at $8,250 gross annually ($117,552.03 in 2020 value). She was doing very well for herself after only three years.

Aunt Daisy faced a tough time when her male customers began to ask for credit to eat. Many of them were the first to be fired from the plants during the Great Depression. She kept her prices reasonable all along and was so grateful for all the tips they garnered her over the previous two years.

She was also thankful for the talks with businesspeople like John Dancy of the Detroit Urban League and Dr. Austin Curtis, Assistant to Dr. George Washington Carver and founder of A.W. Curtis Laboratories in Detroit. He recommended safe methods for her to save, protect, and grow her money through treasury bills and notes, gold, and real estate.

She bought that building at a rock bottom price during the depression under the advice of her friends. She moved upstairs from the back bedroom and only rented out the extra room she stayed in. She kept the kitchen up, continuing to serve breakfast, lunch, and dinner. She fed those who were hungry throughout the depression. When friends had a little extra, they put it in a jar to help those who could not pay. She was part of a great growing community in Detroit. It was a difficult time everywhere, but the community stuck together. All that business ear hustling was paying off. She offered a needed business of quality meals, a room for rent, and a community gathering space.

MR. MUHAMMAD

In the early fall of 1930, a gentleman came in for lunch. Daisy chatted with him, as she did most of her guests, and she learned he was new to town, and he said he was from Mecca. His name was Wallace Fard Muhammad. Muhammad said he came to town for a conference about Black religion and stayed to continue to talk to Black people about Islam and empowerment. Aunt Daisy had heard of Islam, given the large population of Immigrant Muslims in Detroit. Her Islamic customers were mainly male and reluctant to talk to a woman other than getting their food. She had added chicken sausage to her menu to accommodate the many Muslim customers.

Muhammad was more than happy to tell her all about Islam as he ate. He often stayed from breakfast to lunch through closing right into the dinner service, just talking with Daisy and other regulars. She was intrigued by what he was telling her. She had questions about God and Jesus Christ from her upbringing that did not make sense, such as the White Jesus on the crucifix she saw at church. When she learned to read, she was confused that the bible said Jesus's hair was woolly in texture and his feet were like burnished bronze.

Muhammad spoke about Black people rediscovering their true selves, being respected and self-sufficient as well as righteous. He described baby Jesus and Mary symbolically as standing for:

> A woman that was out of the world. She was not a woman of heaven. She was a woman of the world but was chosen by heaven out of the world to bear a child to be sent back into the world to bring back to heaven that particular child that had gone astray and had lost himself in the world. That child is none other than you and I, who was once in the heavenly family belonging to the Holy people, but now gotten ourselves lost in the Western Hemisphere among a strange people; a people that are enemy to us, a people that are not our people, a people that are no friend of ours (Muhammad, E., 1996).

His words took Daisy back to the day in Montgomery when she and her Aunt Dorah narrowly escaped the mob of White men who shot the Black taxi driver.

"Yes," she said as she shook her head. "They are no friends of ours."

Muhammad said he was creating a new movement, and women were essential in it. He was impressed with what she had built and invited her out to hear him speak more.

He frequented her eatery and shared the news of the growth of the "Temple people" (Muhammad, D.Z, 2020), as people called his followers. She offered to bring food to meetings if she came. He recommended she not cook any pork, add whole grains, and limit processed food like white rice, bread, and sugar. She met other women at those meetings, including reconnecting with her friend Lula, who moved out with her husband after having their first baby, and a lady named Mary Almanza, who would become her longtime friend and member of the inner circle of the Temple people. Mary frequented Daisy's eatery with her husband and often took Daisy's cakes and pies to the Temple gatherings.

Daisy occasionally went to the Temple to hear the teachings. She had a business doing well, but she continued to send food to help since many of the people attracted to the Temple were impoverished migrants from the South. In 1931, Mr. Muhammad brought someone to lunch with him. His name was Elijah Poole, then Elijah Karriem, and later named Elijah Mohammed. He was from Georgia but moved to Detroit ten years back with his wife, Clara, and their growing family.

Brother Elijah had only recently met Mr. Muhammad when his wife, Sister Clara, brought him to the Temple, hoping Mr. Muhammad could help her husband overcome his addiction to drinking. Mr. Muhammad spoke very highly of Sister Daisy and her food and encouraged Brother Elijah to introduce his wife, Clara, to Daisy and come back for dinner one evening as his guest. Eventually, Elijah and Clara returned, and they began to talk to Daisy more about the Temple, or the "Nation of Islam" as it was transforming into. They saw the influence she carried in town and wanted her to join them.

Daisy was reluctant to go all-in with the Nation due to the patriarchy she saw the women restricted to. As a business owner, she had more agency and direct control of her life, so she did join over time. She saw why women loved and needed the Nation. Without the Nation, women were vulnerable to sexual advances. Men in the Nation did not objectify them the way non-Muslim men did, and they held them on a pedestal. This was the first time she had seen Black women supported, respected, and admired in her life. The Nation supplied a vehicle for a positive intersection of race, gender, and religion for systematically devalued Black women. Daisy would continue to push herself in business to keep her independence and agency throughout her life as she grew in the Nation.

At one of those sessions at the Temple, as she was bringing in food, she passed by a very handsome man who looked like Cab Calloway, a famous singer, dancer, and bandleader from the era. His name was Henry, but most people called him Brother Henry "10X," because he was the tenth Henry to join the Nation. He was well dressed in black pants, a white shirt, and a black suit jacket. He had nice shoes, too, that were shiny. He held his hat against his chest with his left hand. She noticed his nails were clean, so he didn't work in the factory.

"Sister, please let me get those bags for you," said Brother Henry.

"Thank you," Daisy said.

"How else can I help you?" he asked.

"Um," she stumbled, "I have it from here."

Now Minister Elijah walked up and said, "Perfect, I see you two have met, Sister Daisy. I would like you to meet Brother Henry. He is one of the smartest men I know. He went to college and is a genius at fixing things."

Minister Elijah smiled at them and then walked away, leaving them standing there.

"Pleased to meet you again," Brother Henry said as he held out his hand, waiting for her to shake his.

Men and women were not supposed to shake hands, but she shook his hand and said, "It's very nice to meet you too."

The two of them looked surprisingly bashful for their ages. Daisy continued setting up the meals she brought, and he stayed right there and helped her serve. They made small talk, and she learned he had a degree in Applied Science from Howard University. She was taken aback by his good looks and his intelligence. Daisy was also intrigued that he was not intimidated by her business knowledge, unlike most of the men she met. Most of the men who ate at her eatery thought there was nothing they could offer her. Men would talk shop with her, but she was too much for them to date. Henry was different. He was smooth and worldly. He was just the type of man she needed and wanted, but of course, she did not show it.

Minister Elijah encouraged her to get to know him, and in the early days, he would bring his wife, Sister Clara, and Henry to Daisy's place for dinner. After the second time, she realized they were clearly matchmaking. Mr. Muhammad told her that marriage essentially counts for half of one's faith in Islam.

After nearly a year of attending teachings, she submitted her letter, which was the process for joining the Nation, and a month later, she and Henry were married. He did not move into her house right away. He was respectful and wanted her love to grow for him, so he moved in downstairs. They were married in late 1931, but it seemed more like dating. Dating is not allowed in Islam, so it was refreshing for her to be married but not feel rushed into everything right away, including changing how she dressed. She was always modest with nice dresses that were floor length or tea length below her knee but did not cover her hair until she attended the Temple.

They honeymooned in Idlewild, Michigan, known as "the Black Eden," at the Oakmere Hotel. This was an all-Black resort opened in 1912. They spent their time at the lake, horseback riding, roller skating, eating at the Purple Palace Supper Club, and hobnobbing with other Black vacationers who enjoyed the safe summers there. Toward the end of their stay, they received a telegram saying Grandma Carrie had passed away in Opelika. Daisy and Henry traveled straight away to Alabama in style in their 1931 Ford Model A. The entire family converged back on Opelika. It was quite a sight to see: all the living children of Carrie and George with their grandchildren and great-grandchildren, who Daisy had not seen all together since the summers of the 1920s when all her aunts and uncles shipped their children back to Opelika.

Grandma Carrie, 1926.

Daisy tried to convince Momma to come back with her to Detroit, but she said no because she was the matriarch now with Grandma gone and Dorah, Sarah, Brandt, and Perry still living in Opelika. She did, however, convince Ceola, who was recently single and didn't want to return to Akron. Henry and Daisy returned to Detroit with Ceola and her fourteen-year-old daughter, Bessie. Bessie was a beautiful girl with big brown eyes and honey-colored skin. Daisy was excited to have her sister and niece with her. She was successful but was lonely without her close-knit family nearby.

Henry is a character there is little information about. We don't know his last name and don't have a record of their marriage. He was not a strong figure in the family from the memory of my mother and aunts. He may have been traveling a lot. They do not remember when he died nor what happened to him after Aunt Daisy died.

Aunt Daisy and Uncle Henry 10X. Taken during their travels to Egypt in 1965.

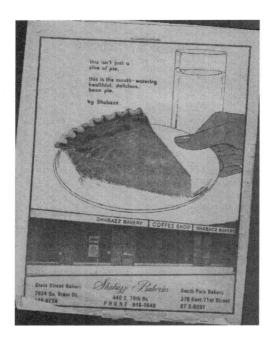

First full-page advertisement of the bean pie in *Muhammad Speaks*, June 5, 1970.

MO-MO TO THE BEAN PIE

Back in Detroit, even through the Great Depression, they had the Eastern Market. Right after World War II, the market boomed in size. On any given weekend, there could have been 20,000 to 30,000 people there, shopping from over 150 different stalls and vendors. Anything in the world could be found at the Eastern Market. Daisy would find food that met the dietary restrictions Mr. Muhammad was teaching. He discouraged sweets, but she was known for her pound cake and sweet potato pie. One of the things he wanted them to eat was the navy bean due to the fiber.

She always had a rebellious spirit, even with her conversion to Islam. She was determined to do more with the navy bean than just boil it and eat it like everybody else. She started making mo-mo with the navy bean, but it did not sell well at the eatery, so she used her foley food press to mash it up and added celery, salt, and garlic to give it more flavor and made a soup. This did very well and became the traditional bean soup of the Nation. But she still wanted and needed something sweet. She always had a sweet tooth. She remixed her sweet mo-mo and made it like a sweet potato pie, including eggs, butter, brown sugar, and some spices to see if this was more palatable than the boiled mo-mo balls. She just called it a bean pie. She served it only to Brother Muhammad first. He accepted it but told her to be mindful of the sugar. She also served it when Minister Elijah and Sister Clara came to dinner. Later, she taught others how to make the bean pie and bean soup and other staple foods as part of Muslim girl training prescribed by Mr. Muhammad with Sister Clara's leadership.

The bean pie is a uniquely Black Muslim delicacy. It's like the Greek baklava. It is quintessentially tasting culture. There are now regional variations in the recipe people make and sell. They can be found gluten-free, vegan, and in a few flavors as well. Today, it is still challenging to find a bean pie unless you are Muslim and someone is still making them at the mosque. There has been limited commercialization of the pie since 1970 when the Nation of Islam (NOI) received Daisy's recipe and began commercializing the sales and production.

Within a few years, the NOI grew to nearly 10,000 people in Detroit. Mr. Muhammad mysteriously disappeared in 1934.

His whereabouts are still a mystery. Aunt Daisy bought two more buildings in Detroit by then and was getting restless, having been there for nine years. All of her aunts and uncles were living in Chicago. She and Minister Elijah were friends, and he confided in her he was preparing to move the entire family to Chicago due to his issues with the government. Authorities jailed him because he refused to put his children in Detroit public schools. He asked if she was interested in moving there and helping him grow the NOI. She had trusted staff to keep the rooming houses managed and depositing the rent each week in the bank in Detroit.

Everyone, including Daisy, Henry, and Ceola, prepared to move to Chicago, but something was not right with Bessie. She was vomiting, and after some prodding from Ceola, she admitted she was seeing a young man named David Richardson, who was also fifteen and from Mississippi. His large family moved to Detroit, as so many other southern families had in the Great Depression, to escape economic and racial oppression. After more digging from Daisy and Ceola, they discovered not only was Bessie seeing the young man, but she was pregnant. As fitting with the time, the families met, and the two young people were wedded. The plans did not change for Daisy. Everyone moved to Chicago, including pregnant Bessie.

RAISING SHIRLEY

Young David visited Chicago during the pregnancy, and on November 10, 1933, Bessie had a healthy baby girl named Shirley. Bessie, however, had a rough labor and delivery for her young age. She was sick off and on during the year after having the baby. Ceola took care of Bessie during her recovery while Daisy cared for baby Shirley. David would make quarterly trips to Chicago and take Bessie out on the town in the hopes of making her feel better. They were married, but he would only stay for short visits then return to Detroit, where he worked and lived with his brother. During his absences, Bessie was sad and anxious without him. She wanted to move to Detroit, but Ceola felt he was not able to support them as just a teen himself. Shirley was a sweet little girl but spoiled, given she had three mommas to choose from. In the fall of 1936, Bessie became ill with pneumonia and never recovered. She died, leaving behind three-year-old Shirley. Ceola and Daisy raised her. Ceola was heartbroken and depressed after the death of her eighteen-year-old daughter, so Daisy took the lead as Shirley's primary caregiver.

Daisy opened a hat shop on 71st and Cottage Grove, not too far from their home. She also managed large events for the NOI, including Savior's Day dinners. Savior's Day is an annual Nation of Islam commemoration of the birth of Master Fard Muhammad on February 26, 1877. Thousands would attend the convention, which had grown to include workshops, health screenings, lively discussions, fashion shows and entertainment, social and educational activities for children and families, and closes with a major address delivered by Minister Elijah Mohammed. Daisy would host a dinner in her large basement. Her meals were legendary. She would make huge vats of fruit salad and serve them in three feet tall marble bowls. She served dignitaries like Muhammad Ali, Louis Farrakhan, the Muhammad family, and other notables invited by the NOI. She took days prepping for the dinners and getting the basement cleaned and decorated. She served fried chicken, fried fish, collard greens, macaroni and cheese, fruit salad, and, of course, bean soup and bean pie.

Over the years, Daisy maintained her high status in the NOI as she devoted time and money to the building of the Nation. Her relationship with Minister Elijah and Sister Clara grew as well. Especially in the early to mid-1940s, as police incarcerated many of the men for violation of draft laws, conspiracy, sedition, and sending their children to cult schools (Lincoln, C., 1973). The FBI and police in Detroit and Chicago kept the NOI under constant surveillance, looking for reasons to arrest them. The women grew closer as they were necessary to lead the Nation. Daisy would spread "dawah," or the act of inviting or calling people to embrace Islam. In her time, they called it fishing but only to family instead of strangers without the men present.

During World War II, with the country at war and concerns about security, the FBI, under J. Edgar Hoover, unleashed a legion of agents to squash any foreign-inspired agitation among American Negroes. The FBI and the Chicago police placed informants within the Nation (then known as the ATOI, Allah Temple of Islam). Their files were some of the only documentation of the Nation's inner workings at that time (Taylor, U., 2017). An FBI informant recounted that Daisy visited her Aunt Dorah in Opelika, Alabama, and shared her religion and continued correspondence in letters. In October 1941, Aunt Dorah and her husband Frank Grand moved to Chicago and took the surname X (Chicago FBI Report, 1942).

Within the family, it made sense that Shirley was raised in the Muslim faith because Ceola had also converted to Islam. Shirley attended Muslim Girl Training (MGT) class that focused on the art of homemaking. It met on weeknights at the Temple and taught how to sew, cook, keep house, rear the children, care for their husbands, and behave at home and abroad (Lincoln, C, 1973). She traveled with Aunt Daisy to other temples in Indiana and Detroit, where she would see her father. They all did their best to bring her up with modesty and grace. Daisy put her in dance lessons, and Shirley did well in school.

Daisy was a strong woman and a domineering figure in everyone's life, but 1942 devastated her and the family. Ceola and Momma Mattie both passed away in Chicago. David attended Ceola's funeral in June. Momma Mattie passed away in November.

David remarried two years before and wanted Shirley to come back to Detroit with him and his wife, Louise. After the repass when everyone was nearly gone, he approached Daisy to talk about his Shirley. "Aunt Daisy, I appreciate you being so gracious to my wife Louise today. She and I have been married for two years now. We have a nice apartment with two bedrooms. I can provide my daughter a good home now." Louise was in the next room with eight-year-old Shirley, playing with dolls. Daisy continued to tidy the room. She glanced up at David and across the room at Louise and Shirley.

"You are not Muslim, David. I have spoken with you before about this. I invited you to the Temple in Detroit, but you refused to come. Shirley is my baby. We raised her. Now

Ceola is gone. She wouldn't want her uprooted. She's too young. You're too young."

"I'm twenty-four, ma'am," David rebutted.

"Well, you should focus on your new life, your wife. Don't you want your own children?" she said.

"I already have a child. And Louise loves Shirley. This is the time for her to come back with us while she is still young and before we have a child to establish us as a family," David urged.

Daisy stood straight up and said, "I disagree with you, David. I don't want to disrupt Shirley. She just lost her grandmother. Her great-grandmother is ill as well. Let's give it some more time. And the issue of our different faiths is not something I can just overlook. We have raised Shirley as a Muslim girl."

David lowered his head. "Aunt Daisy, I appreciate everything you and Ceola did for Bessie and me, helping us raise Shirley since we were so young. My heart broke when Bessie died, but I have a good wife who can be a mother to her. I just want my daughter closer to me."

Daisy responded, "I am a mother to her. I don't want to talk about this anymore. This day has been too much. I just buried my sister."

"You're right. Yes, ma'am," David sighed.

David and Louise went back to Detroit without Shirley. Shirley would visit in the summer, but Daisy would also be in town or nearby vacationing in Idlewild, Michigan. Daisy continued to set the terms of the relationship between David and his daughter. He had a good career in the automobile industry as an engineer, but that did not matter to Daisy. She became more dependent on Shirley as her daughter and assistant as she grew into her teens. The more insistent David would be about Shirley staying in Detroit, the more resistant Daisy would be about her visiting at all. Daisy would keep Shirley busy with her travel schedule and led Shirley to believe it was her father who did not have time for her.

Aunt Daisy visited Alabama in 1940s. She is on the right with the white turban. My Grandmother, Shirley, is the little girl with the big bow.

Daisy's position in the NOI inner circle gave her access. This opened the door to Shirley working with the NOI, reading letters and sometimes drafting responses to keep her busy. Shirley became more rebellious as Daisy forced the teenager to work in the Nation and go to Temple and classes. Shirley would hurriedly pull off her long skirt afterward to show off her legs and go find non-Muslim friends in the neighborhood to hang out with. Shirley then started spending more time at school, and Daisy would have to go there looking for her when no one knew where she was.

Daisy confided in Minister Elijah about what was happening, and he promised to speak to her.

CHICAGO SOUTH SIDE MAP

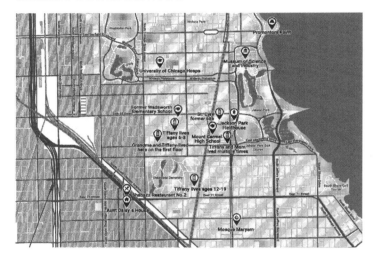

Map of the Chicago South Side highlighting key locations from the book.

PART 2

THE SHIRLEYS

CHAPTER 3

Grandma Shirley

In April of 1951, Shirley was seventeen. Daisy was concerned because Shirley had started coming home later and later. She found her twice coming out of the high school late in the evening. Shirley said she was meeting with a club, but she gave her no details, and the school said no clubs met late, so Shirley said she was with friends. Then Shirley would leave for school and not come home for days at a time. Daisy would go to the school the next day, and Shirley would be there in class. She would wait for her after school and bring her home. The next morning, she would go to school and say she would be home but would disappear again. This went on for a month. She did not know where she was going. She called the police on two occasions, but they were no help. They assured her she was just a loose girl out with some boy. Daisy raised her to be a Muslim girl and could not conceive of her being "loose."

When left alone, Shirley would sneak off. Daisy made sure Auntie Dorah or someone else was watching her. After realizing Shirley had not used any of her feminine supplies in over a month and out of concern for her health, Daisy took her to the doctor. They did a physical, which included a pregnancy test. Daisy was shocked when the nurse told her Shirley was pregnant. They calculated the time from her last cycle and approximated she was four to five weeks pregnant. Daisy thought about calling David but decided against it because he would blame her and want to take her away, so she asked Minister Elijah, whom Shirley respected and admired, to speak with her to see if he could get to the bottom of this.

After much cajoling from Minister Elijah, Shirley told them she was in love with a handsome man, and he was going to marry her. The man's name was Thomas Ross, and he worked at her school. He lived in the community and was in his forties. She had been staying with him after school then at his home. Shirley gave up his address, and Minister Elijah sent three Fruit of Islam (FOI) to the man's home to wait for him. The Fruit of Islam was set up by Fard Muhammad as a military organization within the NOI to protect the organization against unbelievers and, particularly, the police (Lincoln, 1973). He sent the ladies home and said he would follow-up after he had a discussion with this man. After a few hours, they brought Mr. Ross back to the Temple.

Minister Elijah invited him into his office. The FOI stood silently on post in the back of the room. Mr. Ross was very nervous and sweating profusely.

"Why am I here?" he said. "You are holding me here against my will."

"No, sir, my men invited you to the Temple to meet me, and you came. You can leave right now, but I have one question," queried Minister Elijah softly. "Are you in a relationship with a young girl named Shirley Richardson?"

Mr. Ross looked down to the floor then stood up. The brothers stepped up behind him quickly, in unison. Ross turned around, frightened, and sat back down in the chair.

"Miss Richardson is a family friend, and I would like to know the nature of your relationship with her and your intentions," said Minister Elijah.

"I don't know who you are talking about. I am a grown man with three children. What would I be doing with a young girl?" said Mr. Ross.

Minister Elijah looked at him slyly and murmured, "I have some ideas, sir. So, you have no relationship with this girl?"

"I am intending to marry a young woman who grew up across the street from my family, sir," Mr. Ross replied. "Please let me out of here."

"Oh, so you are already engaged. Then you must stay away from this girl. She is with a child. I don't want to have to see you again. Do you understand?" Minister Elijah sternly exclaimed.

Minister Elijah waved his hand. The brothers stood back and opened the door. Mr. Ross stood and practically bolted out the door.

The next day Minister Elijah asked Daisy back to his office. She left Shirley at home with Brother Henry watching her.

"That man denied knowing her. He does not want to marry her. He has intentions with another woman," he told Daisy.

Daisy began to tear up. "This was like Bessie all over again. Why would she do this?" she mumbled. "You know she always needed her father, and she seemed to be getting one in the wrong ways. This is my fault for pushing her father away," said Daisy.

"Sister Daisy. It's too late for that now. I assure you Mr. Ross won't be coming around her again, but we must fix this situation. You are to find a young man to marry Sister Shirley," said Minister Elijah.

They sat down right then, and Daisy discussed a few young men in their circle of family friends. Minister Elijah shot down any of the young men in the Nation because the fallout from anyone finding out the truth would cause dissension in the ranks of the members. For Daisy's sake and the Nation's, he recommended she look at other young men not in the Nation but who Shirley knew from the neighborhood or school.

Daisy went home and told Shirley about Mr. Ross's denial of her and their relationship. Shirley was distraught Mr. Ross denied knowing her. She thought he loved her. Now she was hurt and wanted to hurt him back. Aunt Daisy shared the plan of finding a suitable husband for her. She asked for a few names of young men Shirley might consider marrying. At first, Shirley was against this. Daisy said the other option was for her to go away to abort the baby. She did not want that, so she relented. The young man she liked most was Wilbur Green. He was a young man who lived on the next block over from them. He and Shirley grew up together and had gone to the same schools their entire life, and he had a crush on her. The families knew each other well and often celebrated their birthdays, November 10 and 12, together.

Daisy invited his mother, Lillie, over for Sunday dinner. Shirley was polite and gave him an opening to court her. Wilbur always loved Shirley and fell right in line. She did not tell him she was pregnant, so their courtship was very short. On May 28, 1951, Wilbur and Shirley were married in a beautiful ceremony.

Shirley was elegant in her wedding dress, and her cousin, Mattie Renee, stood by her side. She looked as though she was forcing herself to try to smile. It's understandable why. This was a "shotgun wedding," and maybe only those two young ladies and Daisy knew why. David and Louise were invited and attended but were also kept in the dark about the truth.

Shirley gave birth to Wilbur "Sweetie" Green on January 16, 1952. She and Wilbur had an outwardly good marriage, but she was not in love with him. She was still pining for the unattainable Mr. Ross. She knew he was too old for her, but he made her feel special in a way Wilbur could not and did not know how to do. Ross stayed away for a time. He got married on October 1, 1951, and his wife had a baby in March 1952. He broke his promise and came looking for Shirley again. Shirley got away to see him even with them both married with babies, and soon after, she was pregnant again.

Cousin Mattie Renee and Shirley at her wedding in 1951.

A DNA test done in 2021 confirmed Mr. Ross was the father of this child as well. She gave birth to Shirley Green on January 13, 1953, when she was nineteen. Shirley's relationship with Wilbur became more contentious because she gave birth to another child who looked nothing like him. They were rarely intimate, so he questioned if the child was his.

Speculation began within Wilbur's family that Sweetie nor little Shirley were his children because both were of light complexion. Wilbur was very dark-skinned. This is not unusual in Black families, but Sweetie had hazel eyes, which is unusual because no one else in his family has anything but brown eyes. Wilbur grew angry because Shirley was always leaving the children with him or Aunt Daisy. When Wilbur spoke up about this, Shirley tried to smooth things over by being intimate with him. Wilbur eventually gave in, recognizing those children were not his as they got a little older. Shirley knew her marriage was a lie and had been with Wilbur long enough not to bring any embarrassment to the family. Wilbur and Shirley parted ways in 1954 after three years of marriage. Wilbur remarried later in life and had one daughter, Latonya. He never spoke of the true nature of his marriage with Shirley to his daughter, nor did he look for Wilbur Jr. or Shirley even though he lived his entire life in the Chicago metropolitan area. He passed away in 2012.

FROM THE POT TO THE FRYING PAN

Shirley met Jesse "Sonny" Boyd in an elevator while she was on an errand for Aunt Daisy in the winter of 1953. She was still married to Wilbur, but she was very attracted to this handsome man. He was tall, at six feet two inches, and was well dressed in a hat and overcoat.

Jesse was not very educated, but he was sweet, good-looking, charismatic, and from Alabama. He initially used this to get Daisy comfortable with his ability to take care of Shirley and her two children. After she and Wilbur divorced, she married Jesse "Sonny" Boyd when she was twenty years old in the living room of 611 E. 71st, a four-room apartment in a two-flat Aunt Daisy owned. Shirley moved in there after she left Wilbur. Aunt Daisy was always there to pick up the pieces.

Jesse Boyd Jr. was born in 1929 in Birmingham, Alabama. He had a difficult childhood as the oldest of five siblings. His father was Jessie Willie Boyd, and his mother was named Velma Davis. They were very poor and moved from

Birmingham to Cincinnati, Ohio, but it was during the depression that the Ohio River overflowed, and there were no jobs for his father. His mother took the three youngest to Chicago, but Jesse Willie came and got them. They put the children in an orphanage after his two youngest siblings burned down the house playing with fire. The welfare workers found out the father was working and there was no mother present. After a day, Jesse Willie got them out and took them back to Alabama. His mother was a drug addict and stayed in Chicago. His father raised them all as a single man, which is where his passion for fatherhood came from. Jesse's father was killed by one of his lovers in 1951.

Shirley and Jesse went on to have six more children (five girls and a stillborn boy) in addition to Wilbur and Shirley:

Deborah "Debbie"—October 12, 1955
Valerie—August 12, 1956
Delovely "DeDe"—December 27, 1958
Melody—December 12, 1960
Robbin—May 12, 1962

Although Jesse was in and out of jail, he always came home. He did his best to take care of his family, but he was on heroin, unbeknownst to Shirley when they first met. Like many Black men of the era, he had limited opportunities, so he did illegal things that landed him in jail, such as dealing drugs and burglary. Over time he became more controlling and abusive to Shirley and beat her in his drug-induced rages. After so many babies back-to-back, Shirley decided to get a tubal ligation in 1963 so she could not have any more pregnancies. While in recovery, she received morphine at the hospital.

When she went home, she was still suffering from depression and an abusive husband. Without access to the prescribed pain medications to keep her numb, she needed something to take the edge off. It was at this point Jesse introduced her to heroin to subdue her. He brought her into his drug world, and she became an addict.

The family was furious at Jesse for the abuse, but they didn't know about the drug use. They wanted Shirley to stop letting him back in when he got out of jail. Like most abused women, she did not want anyone's help, including her children or family. It took some time for them to realize her drug addiction. The house went into disrepair when it was usually impeccable, and she slept all day even though she had five little girls. David, who visited his grandchildren, often recognized something more was wrong and approached Daisy about the state of the home. As Shirley had more children, Daisy didn't go over there as often, so she wasn't aware of it until David brought it up. It broke their hearts to see her so out of her mind.

The death of her mother at three, then her grandmother and great-grandmother at eight were so significant and painful it stunted her emotional development (Haine et al., 2008), and she had short-term (Rostila and Saarela, 2011) and long-term consequences for her mental health (Ellis et al., 2013). Shirley's grandmother, Ceola, and Aunt Daisy provided continuity within the same home. They also supported her young father, David, by supporting her long-term care. They included her in the Nation of Islam as a network of safety and community until her adolescent hormonal and mental changes made her vulnerable to seduction from an older man, pushing her into adulthood, parenthood, and marriage. These studies speak of the long-term implications of bereaved children as adults becoming drug addicts, having emotional and physical abuse, joblessness, and a higher disposition on women than men. Shirley hurt in ways no one could see, and even with all the support, she still was vulnerable and would continue to suffer from trauma and pass it on to her children.

After Aunt Daisy passed away in 1969, Shirley received Aunt Daisy's home in her will, and Jesse and their children moved from the two-bedroom flat at 611 E. 71st Street to Daisy's larger home at 619 E. 71st Street. After settling her affairs, Shirley and Jesse liquidated all of Daisy's assets in Chicago, Ohio, Indiana, and Alabama. They took years of Daisy's hard work and savings, and in too short a time, liquidated the money and properties to use the money largely for drugs.

Shirley's first grandchild was me, Tiffany. I was born in 1976 to her oldest daughter, Shirley, and she offered to take care of me while my mother worked. My momma told her she had to get clean first. Grandma went into a treatment program that included the use of methadone, and she was clean by the time I was nine months old. This was the first time she was clean since 1963. It gave her joy to have a second chance to do things better with her granddaughter.

The home Aunt Daisy built also went into disrepair, then the pipes froze and burst in the winter of 1978. Shirley was not paying the taxes on the house either. She abruptly moved her and her younger daughters into public housing, "the projects" called the Robert Taylor Homes, in 1979. Everyone went except my momma and me. We started staying with other family members. The family moved in the projects from 1979–1981. This was right on the heels of the crack epidemic, but the community was still in tack, and families were not devastated yet. Many people were coming over because Valerie and Robbin were teens, and Melody went to the army in August 1981. Granddaddy Jesse was around, but he did not live there consistently. Grandma lived on the fifteenth floor, so everyone looked like ants from the breezeway up there. Grandma and Granddaddy seemed to be friends by that time. She grew up and was not allowing him to abuse her physically. He was still providing for the family. Granddaddy Jesse would drive an ice cream truck and take me with him. He sold ice cream all over the South Side.

At the Robert Taylor Homes, there were at least fifty other children at any given time on the playground. The housing authority fed the children meals, and we did arts and crafts in the multipurpose room on the ground floor. The kids had their own world in the projects. Children were away from the gaze of parents, so typically, older siblings and cousins controlled what was happening on the playground. There were good times there. I would be with my aunts, who were teenagers then. I went with Auntie DeDe to a tiny record store across the street, and she bought Sugar Hill Gang's *Rapper's Delight* album. I remember the sky-blue cover and my aunts playing the song repeatedly. I knew it by heart, and I was five.

Grandma got Section 8 in 1981, which is a housing voucher given by the public housing authority. With the voucher, Grandma moved into the Woodlawn neighborhood in a huge top-floor apartment on East 64th Street near Greenwood beside the old Wadsworth Elementary School the summer before I started first grade there. My mom used to wake me up early in the morning and take me on the bus to Grandma's for school, but that was hard on both of us. So, midway through first grade, I began living with Grandma during the week and staying with my momma on the weekends.

The apartment was big with three bedrooms. Robbin and Valerie stayed there, as did anyone else when they needed to. Uncle Sweetie was also staying there off and on. It was the family home, and we would have dinners and Christmas there. I remember once when Auntie Melody came back from the army in Oklahoma. A guy she was dating knew the block but not the building. I woke up that morning hearing someone screaming, "Melody, Melody!" down at the street. I woke her and let her know someone was looking for her.

When I was nine, Grandma moved to the other side of the school on 65th and Greenwood. My mother moved next door to her after a year. I was seeing and understanding more as I got older. The drug abuse was apparent due to increasing traffic of people in and out of Grandma's house, loud music, and arguments.

Even with the drug issue going on, Grandma still had a big part in raising me as well as my other little cousins as they came along. I have memories of listening to music and dancing with her in the living room, especially to Motown and Smokey Robinson. She had this burgundy velvet furniture set, fancy record player, and radio set with a floor model television. We spent a lot of time watching television with her. I danced to Michael Jackson during the Motown 25 in 1983 in her living room.

People might view her as having lived a poor life. She was financially supported all her life by her husband, her children, and welfare. I never knew her to work outside of the house. She was a homemaker, and she kept a clean home, and she taught me how to clean. She was also a good cook. She loved to barbecue. She could be sweet, and she had a good sense of humor. But I had to learn how to watch for her mood swings. If she locked herself in her bedroom, she was getting high, and I would stay away. She could be either overly sweet or mean in that state of mind. A small thing could set her off—especially if she did not get her way. I guess I learned emotional intelligence at a young age from her.

Aunt Robbin was the youngest of my aunties. She was a pretty girl, but because no one encouraged her to stay in school, she lived a street life and had street smarts over book smarts. She was dating a big-time drug dealer when we were living on Greenwood. He would roll up in his fancy Cadillac and sit on the hood in front of the building. He would sell drugs to people on the block and give drugs to Grandma. I only know because one day he left, and I heard a lot of yelling from across the hall. I snuck and put my ear on Grandma's front door to hear what was happening.

"Momma, that's enough!" screamed Robbin.

"Don't you tell me what to do. He told me I could have whatever I wanted. I want the rest of what he gave you!" exclaimed Shirley.

"But that's not all for you. That's for me to make a sale, and I have to give him a certain amount of money back," cried Robbin.

Shirley demanded, "He won't care. Just give it to me."

"No, you don't need anymore, Momma. No," said Robbin.

Everyone had a front porch, so I could also hear and see everything by sitting there. I heard screaming and running around inside Grandma's house. I heard someone coming near the door, so I ran back inside our apartment. As soon as I did, the door swung open, and I could hear Grandma and Robbin arguing in the hallway. I went to our porch and then heard the building door *eeek* open.

Robbin was yelling at Grandma, saying, "No, I am not giving you anything else!"

Grandma went into her house and came right back out. Robbin screamed and took off, running down the street. Grandma had a knife and was chasing after her, demanding more drugs. This was a saddening and violent site for me to witness. It changed me and how I saw the disease called drug addiction. My aunt tried to do what she could to make her mother happy, but it would never be enough. I was twelve at the time. I am grateful my mother was not there. She must have been at work.

Drugs were a problem in our family, just like so many families around us, even in the building. There was another family, the Greens (no relation), who lived above my mother. The mother, Ms. Green, lived there with her four sons. One of them, Amos, married my Aunt Valerie. They are still together. At least three of the other Green sons were on drugs or are alcoholics. Our families are close, and I have so much respect for the love between Valerie and Amos. She keeps every single teddy bear, valentine card, and chocolate box he has ever given her. They are on the wall of their bedroom. It is a monument to their love that has overcome drug abuse, poverty, death, and anything else life has thrown at them. We don't see enough of that sort of love in our family.

Eventually, cardiac arrest from drugs killed my grandma when she overdosed while taking a bath in 1992. I was sixteen. I am sad to say at the time, I felt relieved when she died, because my relationship with her was more difficult as I got older. I was aware of her drug addiction and the terror she caused within the family and could no longer be a victim of it. My mother was depressed a lot from seeing her mother on drugs since she was a child but also from the lack of love she showed her throughout her life. I see now why that may have been the case. I also have a deeper understanding of the trauma my grandma went through losing her mother at age three and being victimized by an older man, hiding the true father of her oldest children, marrying a man she didn't love, being abused by her second husband, and becoming addicted to drugs. The effect of those traumas is long-lasting and has rippled into the next generations.

Granddaddy died in 2002 from a brain aneurysm. He was struggling with drugs late into his life. When he passed away, we finally met his other set of children, and the oldest was four years younger than me. Ebony, Tamika, Robert, and Chris have been a part of the family since that time. It is no big deal they have a different mother. Broken apart since being torn from Africa, African American families have learned family is family and to recreate family structure repeatedly. Grandma knew about the other woman and his other four children. This was probably why he was in and out of her house, and eventually they broke up completely.

VENERATION

My grandma was a woman who suffered many traumas, starting with her mother's death at three, an absentee father, inappropriate relationships, teenage pregnancies, physical abuse, and drug addiction. She longed for a closer relationship with her father, which could have prevented so much of her divergent behavior.

The twenty-five-year age difference between my grandma and Mr. Ross was notable. The relationship was unacceptable and displayed by her neglect of her eldest children, Sweetie and Shirley. We may never know the true dynamic of this adult man's entanglement with my teenage grandmother. I can conjure questions like, Was this a consensual relationship? Was grandma angry she had to marry Wilbur Green? Did she marry Wilbur to make Mr. Ross jealous? Was she angry Mr. Ross married someone else who had a baby two months after her son? Were her children conceived in love? Why did she act as if she did not care about them and their well-being?

I often look at the wedding photo of Grandma and cousin Mattie Renee. They were close until they were adults. They raised their children together, and their lives took similar paths but diverged in terms of religion and trauma. Grandma never went to a mosque or church or raised her children with a spiritual foundation. They both went on to have large families. Mattie Renee brought her children up in the Christian church and away from drugs and street life. Mattie Renee had six children—Sharon "Dottie," the twins, Carla "Jowan" and Arla "Joann," Fatima "Tina," Robert "Pig," and Marcus "Bay."

In the spring of 2020, I attended a virtual celebration given by Mattie Renee's children and grandchildren to honor the twelfth year of her passing. It occurred to me listening to them all that my family had never honored my grandma in any way, and that hurt me. Not just for me but for my mother, for my son who never got to meet his great-grandmother. Despite her troubles, I know she would have doted on him and fussed over him the way his grandmother does.

I don't want my grandma remembered because of her troubles. Therefore, I wanted to know more about her story because "hurt people hurt people." I needed to know why the bubbly young lady in the exquisite wedding dress became a drug addict and why she was angry most of the time. She was a beautiful and funny lady who could charm anyone with her smile. She tried to be a good mother, and cooking came honest to her. She was close to her daughters in the best of times, and she would fight with them in the worst of times, but that's common to most families. Everyone loved her, though. She looked out for me, attended parent conferences, came to all my school events, and did the best she could.

Ms. Shirley in her prime.

She may not have shown my mother love in a traditional way, but maybe through taking care of me, she tried to show it or make up for what she missed or could not do for my mother. Her traumas left her without the ability to show love and self-medicated to push down the pain. I thank her for taking care of me while my mother worked. I know she loved me, and I loved her. I honor her through the questions I ask. I honor her through the answers I have discovered and those I may never fully understand.

I venerate her with these words.

CHAPTER 4

Little Shirley

—

It is only known in the present that my mother was born into a shotgun marriage to hide the inappropriate pregnancy between my grandma and a man old enough to be her father. My mother heard the whispers through her adolescence that Wilbur Green was not her father, and they were correct but only confirmed through the science of DNA. She lost the man, Wilbur Green, thought to be her father through divorce, and her mother remarried Jesse Boyd when she was two years old. Jesse Boyd was not a consistent father figure, either, due to his lifestyle in the early marriage as a gangster and criminal. My grandmother was herself a young woman reeling from the bereavement of her mother at age three and her grandmother and great-grandmother at age eight. Those traumas had a lasting impact on her development and continued to affect her ability to show care and tenderness toward her own children. My grandma's psychopathology or features of her mental health considered collectively may be why she was a depressive, manic, drug-addicted person as an adult and why she could not be a more outwardly caring mother. I have always wondered what my grandmother thought about her relationship with her daughter. Did she long to hold her and be more tender, but something prevented her?

I have also thought about the extreme scenario about Thomas Ross, the older man with whom she was involved and my biological grandfather. Could they have been in love, was my grandmother just a teenage girl in love but it was one-sided, or was he just a pedophile seducing vulnerable teenage girls? I always come back to him seducing her, because she was angry and neglected my mother and my uncle. It took a lot of coaxing to get my mother to tell much of what I will write about her in this chapter. I am grateful for her sharing because it deepened my understanding of her and her mother's relationship and shed light on my relationship with her as an adolescent. Our relationship now is much closer and more understanding, given our journey together to write this book. I heard the pain in my mother's voice as she spoke about her mother. She had not spoken about her mother to anyone, not even a therapist. It was painful for her to relive it all, but I asked her to trust me. I wanted to help her understand and forgive her mother if possible. I wanted to find the root of the pain to show my mother that Grandma was also in pain and her actions were not malice. What my mother shared initially about my grandma expanded my need for more information about the family and made me want answers, more so for her than for me.

Momma said, "I didn't like being in my mother's house."

Momma was most happy when she was outside. Inside the house, she feared the fighting between her mother and "daddy" (her stepfather, Jesse "Sonny" Boyd) because the abuse caused her mother to stay hurt physically and mentally. Momma told me about when they would have company at the house and Granddaddy would hit Grandma and knock her out of the chair in front of their guests. When Momma tried to protect Grandma, she would get angry with her. Her mother slept all day and made my mother cook and clean for her little sisters as they came along. Grandma took it out more on her and her brother because Jesse was gone most of the time running the streets. She tried to prevent them from going out and accomplishing their goals. She did not understand why her mother could not show love to her and her brother. She would sneak out while Grandma slept on the couch.

A blue sofa and 1960s style tables and chairs furnished the apartment. They lived in the two flat Aunt Daisy owned. After Aunt Daisy died, they moved into her house, which was a big, nice house Aunt Daisy had built around 1950. Momma spent more time there, anyway. She described a trap door that allowed you to get from the house to the basement without going outside. Aunt Daisy kept preserves down in the basement, and she had a washer and dryer. Grandma did not know that until she moved into the house. Aunt Daisy had never told them because she did not want Grandma coming to use it to wash Jesse's clothes. Momma said, "Aunt Daisy was 'stingy' and didn't want your grandma bringing all Granddaddy's things over to her house and breaking her machines. So, your grandma went to the laundromat to wash and most of the time sent me until I got old enough to start working."

I imagine Aunt Daisy would have to be stingy to keep any money, given Grandma and Granddaddy's drug issue. Aunt

Daisy would pay my momma a few dollars to dust the house to earn some money. Aunt Daisy wanted Momma to be more independent, which is probably what gave her the idea to stay on the lookout for a job for her.

When Momma was in seventh grade, she and her friend, Caroline Marshbank, signed up for Hirsh High School typing course in the summer. It was a free class. She learned on a manual typewriter. By the end of the summer, she could type fifty to sixty words per minute. She thought she probably signed the permission slip for her mother. The class was two to three days per week for a few hours.

Anytime Momma was genuinely happy about something, Grandma would stand in the way or try to prevent it. Momma was a ping-pong champion. Grandma would not allow her to attend. Perhaps she wanted her to stay home and be miserable with her. Momma went anyway and snuck out of the house to attend the championship. She started playing ping-pong at thirteen in the neighborhood at South Park on 71st and King Drive. She played for years. I suggested recently she pick it back up as a way of staying active.

She also wanted to be a majorette with the Elks Lodge, but Grandma would not let her march. Aunt Daisy bought her the uniform, boots, and baton, but Grandma still would not let her. She allowed her other children, especially the next oldest, Deborah "Debbie," to do anything she wanted from the perspective of Momma. This underscores the residue of what Grandma may have been feeling about her relationship with Mr. Ross and being overwhelmed with many children.

Little Shirley in high school.

Aunt Daisy always took my mother and Uncle Sweetie to the mosque with her. Aunt Daisy would have her and Sweetie change clothes at her house, and then they would go to the mosque. She would never take clothes from Aunt Daisy's house. She wore long skirts and scarves. Aunt Daisy would show her and Sweetie off to everyone there. Momma always felt there was something unsaid in how she and her brother were treated by Aunt Daisy versus their mother. I can now imagine Aunt Daisy was trying to compensate for her niece's ill behavior toward her older children. She also did not want to trigger my Grandma Shirley and prevent her from having access to my mother if she knew she was taking her to the mosque, given her turning away from being a Muslim. Momma would also travel with Aunt Daisy to the mosque in South Bend, Indiana, where she had a house and helped establish a Temple.

MOMMA CARRIES THE BEAN PIE RECIPE

It was 1967, and Momma—only fourteen at the time—sat on Aunt Daisy's mint green house front porch eating a piece of bean pie. She stretched her legs out in front of her, her tan skin gleaming in the sun. She had pulled her short, natural hair back into a ponytail as she wore it most days. Aunt Daisy's bean pie is made of navy beans, spices, butter, sugar, and vanilla, so it is more than a dessert. It could be breakfast, lunch, or a dessert. Momma watched as Aunt Daisy and Uncle Ten (Henry) came out of Shabazz Restaurant, which was directly across the street from the house.

Aunt Daisy told Momma Brother Robert, the manager, was looking for a new waitress now that Belinda intended to marry Muhammad Ali. Aunt Daisy had essentially settled things and gotten Momma the job, but to start working, Aunt Daisy told Brother Robert she was sixteen. They walked over to the restaurant and made introductions as Brother Robert explained the responsibilities of the job. Thus began my mother's relationship of working at Shabazz Restaurant. She worked there from ages fourteen to nineteen, from 1967 to 1972.

Not long after Momma began working at Shabazz, she was on her lunch break eating bean pie from Aunt Daisy.

"Hey, Sister Shirley, do you mind asking Sister Daisy if she will share that bean pie recipe with me?" asked Brother Robert.

"Okay, sure, I'll go ask her," Shirley replied as she bounced off the stool, ran out the door and across the street. She ran into the front door, straight into the kitchen where Aunt Daisy was.

"Miss, aren't you supposed to be at work?" Aunt Daisy prodded.

"I am at work, but Brother Robert asked me to ask you if he could have the recipe for your bean pie," Shirley spat out in one breath.

Aunt Daisy looked down, patted her roast, then put it in the oven. She wiped her hands on her apron and walked over to a box on the counter, opening it to take out a pencil and paper. She sat down and wrote out the recipe for the bean pie, then handed it to little Shirley.

"You want me to give him any instructions?" asked Shirley.

"He's been cooking for twenty years. He can figure it out. You can taste one and tell him if it's right or not. He knows where I live." She turned around and went right on cooking her dinner.

Momma ran back across the street and handed the recipe to Brother Robert. Soon after, the restaurant was making the pies. The Nation of Islam, which owned the restaurant since the 1930s, only began selling bean pies in 1970 and refers to them as "by Shabazz."

In the 1960s, Black people could not eat just anywhere. This restaurant was also where Black people on the South Side of Chicago ate, including musicians like the Temptations, movie stars, athletes like Muhammad Ali, leaders like Farrakhan, and other notables in Chicago. The restaurant had seats around the counter as soon as you walked in. If the brothers were alone, they would sit at the counter, but if they came in with their family, they would ask to sit in the dining room. If they wanted to have a party, they would have to reserve the dining room. Momma was a personal waitress for many parties. Her fondest memory was waiting on famous people like Cassius Clay, a.k.a. Muhammad Ali. She also would go with Brother Robert to cater at the Regal Theater when it was on 47th and King Drive. Once, they catered for the Temptations, and she was able to be backstage.

Momma had a strong work ethic, but she almost dropped out of high school to work more. She did not think her mother cared whether she went to school or not, and she wished she had someone to encourage her to go to college. She was an avid reader of Black history and Black authors during that time. She was constantly reading even through my childhood. Momma aspired to be a math teacher—unbeknownst to me. I never once in my life knew my mother loved math or wanted to be a teacher, but she never had anyone to push her to finish school, so she lost interest. She had no knowledge of college, how to get in, or financial aid. Only three of Grandma's seven children finished high school. Something told her to finish school, and a school counselor encouraged her to finish. She was lucky to graduate from high school. No one told her she was smart. But she knows now she was smart. She planned even at a young age to instill education in her children. She made sure her children would have exposure to books and programs. She put us in educational programs even when she could not afford it. She always found a way.

MORE THAN A SISTER

At the age of twenty, Momma understood more than her sisters ever would how it felt to be uncared for by their mother. She did not want that for them and tried her best to protect them from the abuse and neglect she felt from their mother, my grandma. Her sisters were between ten and sixteen at that time.

She would take her little sisters out and buy them an outfit every week, one by one. She would also take them out to Ronnie's steakhouse on Wabash as part of their outing. Taking children to get clothes was something her mother should have been doing, but Momma was a caring big sister trying to fill the gap left by Grandma, who was incapacitated most days from drugs, depression, or domestic abuse. Momma did these weekly shopping trips and lunch dates within enough time each summer before school started, so all her five little sisters had one new outfit to wear on the first day of school. She wanted them to feel good about themselves.

After high school, Momma could not find a full-time job, and Shabazz was only part-time and not enough to support herself, but she knew how to type. She learned about the Job Corps from a poster in the employment office. She applied and got accepted to the Job Corps for Women. She started at age nineteen in 1972 and went to Cleveland, Ohio, for the program, which lasted nine months. This was her first time away from home. Her roommates were Janice and Elaine. She is still friends with Janice. Their birthdays were only three days apart. They keep in touch on Facebook now, and she visits her in Chicago.

In the Job Corps, she learned secretarial work. She got a spending allowance every three months to buy toiletries. She had not experienced freedom so far from home, and most of the time she was goofing off, so she got kicked out. She came home in the spring.

Momma knew she had messed up a good opportunity by getting kicked out of Job Corps, but at least she could use the $125 check to pay for her expenses, so she kept calling the office asking about the check. She just happened to go to the liquor store on 71st and St. Lawrence around the corner from the house for a drink. She was talking with the owner, whom everyone in the neighborhood knew well and chatted with when they went into the store.

"Hey, little Shirley, I haven't seen you since last winter!" the store owner said.

"I was away at Job Corps, but I am back now but just waiting on a check for a hundred and twenty-five dollars from them," she mentioned.

"Really? That's a nice amount for a young lady. A hundred and twenty-five dollars, you don't say," he paused. "Wait a minute... I just cashed a check for $125 from the Job Corps a few days ago your mother brought in," he blurted out.

Momma was red in the face and could barely respond. "Thanks for telling me." She walked out and marched home.

She bolted through the front door.

"Momma, the man at the store said you cashed my check from Job Corps…" Momma's chest was going up and down from nearly running to the house. But Grandma was silent.

"Momma, do you hear me?" Momma said again.

"Yeah, I heard you, girl. Yeah, so what? I cashed the check. What do you need the money for, anyway?"

She was gone for months and forgot how mean her Momma could be for no reason. Why would she take the money she had earned? She knew she would not get the money back. She would not even give her the pleasure of asking. Momma felt dejected and disappointed. She was angry she even used the house for her address. She could not look at her mother. Momma left and moved in with Janice's family after that. Momma's friends have been a secondary family throughout her life, and this would not be the last time she would need to count on her friends over her family.

Momma's next job was at Uaaro, a paper company. She worked in the office putting in orders. She was the only African American and the first in the office due to Affirmative Action. Affirmative action itself is "any measure, beyond simple termination of a discriminatory practice, adopted to correct or compensate for past or present discrimination or to prevent discrimination from recurring in the future."

(US Commission on Civil Rights, Statement on Affirmative Action, 1977.) Therefore, affirmative action means taking positive steps to end discrimination, prevent its recurrence, and create new opportunities previously denied to minorities and women.

A White girl in the company used to bring in food and nuts, and Momma thought the girl was her friend until she overheard her describe the nuts as "nigga nuts" and laugh about it. Momma went to her boss and reported the girl was creating a hostile work environment. The girl was brought into the office and reprimanded for her behavior but not fired. Momma never spoke to her again. The business was on 63rd and Western. She worked there a couple of years until she got pregnant with me.

Momma lived in an apartment with a boyfriend, but she found out he was taking the rent money to buy drugs. Momma then decided to move back to Grandma's house. She bought Grandma a beautiful cocktail table, hoping she would show some kindness to her, but she never got what she wanted from her mother. Grandma mentally could not show kindness toward Momma. I have to believe it was the trauma, because thinking she was intentionally hurting her daughter makes me angry, and I know my Grandma was not that type of person.

MEETING MY DAD

One night Momma and Janice decided to go to a bar for a drink since they had just turned twenty-one. A young man sat next to Momma at the bar.

"You are very pretty," said the man.

She responded, "You look okay."

They kept talking, and he let her know he worked for Amtrak for two years. He was from Wynne, Arkansas, and his name was Vernest Cantrell. They were both twenty-one. They began dating. She would meet him in his hotel room since he was always traveling with Amtrak. He was a porter and did not have a car. After dating for a time, when he got into town, he would come and stay with her at Grandma's. He did not like the way Grandma talked to Momma. She was nice enough to him because he was giving her money.

In the Spring of 1975, Momma felt different and had missed her cycle. She went to Planned Parenthood, and they confirmed she was pregnant. This was her first pregnancy. It was an easy pregnancy with no morning sickness. She craved grapes—especially wine grapes that are available in August.

On January 27, 1976, she went to her last doctor checkup. She was babysitting her best friend Barbara's son, Tanzel, who was three, and Auntie Debbie was with her. The doctor said she had preeclampsia and told her to go straight to Billings Hospital at the University of Chicago. They induced her labor, but it took thirty-six hours before they performed a C-section because her cervix did not dilate. She did not get to see me until the next day. The nurses initially brought in a dark-skinned baby, and although she had not seen me, she knew they had the wrong baby. She was very vocal about it, and they eventually corrected their mistake and brought me in to see her. My father was on the road when I was born. Momma said he was being an "asshole." He eventually came around to see me when he got back in town, but he would not sign my birth certificate. He was afraid his parents would find out he had a baby out of wedlock.

She went on public assistance for four months because she could not work. She found a job working at Montgomery Wards office on Chicago Avenue near the Cabrini Green projects that May. She was a good word processing operator with super-fast typing speeds, so finding a job was not very difficult if they were open to hiring someone Black. Grandma was keeping me when she went to work. She told Grandma she had to get off drugs to keep me. People would be at the house, and she told her again. Grandma really loved me and having a baby around again. She went to a clinic and was prescribed methadone as part of the treatment. It took her a while, but by the time I was nine months, she was clean.

Momma was still staying with Grandma and did not know she was not paying taxes on Aunt Daisy's house until she abruptly told everyone they needed to move into the projects. She never told her how much the back tax bill was. Momma told her she was not moving into the projects with me. The day she found out they were moving to the projects, she was only able to put our things into two garbage bags. Momma called Cousins Dottie and Jowan to stay at the Scaife/Griffin family building on 1534 E. 65th place. She took our bags, and we slept in the dining room there on a couch. She took me off the bottle of carnation milk, Karo syrup, and baby vitamins because I was over a year old. It was hard to be "homeless" and keep up with the formula.

She had nowhere else to go, so she dealt with not having any privacy and their late nights of playing cards and partying while we were sleeping nearby.

Momma put me in daycare at the Underwoods place on 72nd and Champlain. She took me by bus there and then took the bus to Montgomery Wards. Mr. Underwoods saw a young lady trying hard to make it, so he started picking me up to make it easier for her to go straight to work. She began looking for another job that made more money to get a place of her own.

She found a job at CNA Insurance while still living at 65th place. She started in October 1977 as a word processing operator. I was eighteen months old. CNA has good benefits. Her title was Word Processor Operator for ten years, then Licensing Technician for ten years. I remember visiting that red building in downtown Chicago many times throughout my life. Momma could type so fast. She could hold an entire conversation with you and keep typing whatever document she was working on. It is amazing to think about the change in jobs from then and now. People can now do everything she was doing with a computer, but she was called a word processor. I loved visiting her at work. All her coworkers would be so nice to me, and I could get candy off their desks. I have so much respect for my mom and how hard she worked to support me. In 1977–78, Black women made less than $9,377 per year on average while White women made $9,900 annually. When she retired in 2000, she was making $43,000 per year. When I came out of college in 1998, I was making at least $40,000. She was overworked and underpaid.

She met Ronnie Jones at CNA. They became fast friends. She was bubbly and cheerful. She lived around the corner from the family building on 65th and Marquette. She told Momma she needed a roommate. We moved in with Ronnie and her daughter, also named Tiffany, but she was a few years older than me. Momma and I walked across the lot to the new apartment. Ronnie and Momma split the bills. That was a good time. Momma had a good job, and she and I were finally happy and settled. My dad would stay over and moved in with us. Ronnie wanted both to pay rent for the same room. Then Ronnie's boyfriend moved in, which signaled it was time to go.

Momma found an apartment on 69th and Calumet. Her friend's sister referred her there. It was a three-bedroom, which was too big just for us to afford, so my Auntie Valerie, her boyfriend Michael, and their son Devoy lived with us. Earnest, my dad's twin brother, got out of the service and came to live with us.

It was at this time my dad started dating another woman named Mary. She was a bold one and came to the apartment and said she was his girlfriend. He and my mother were clearly living together. Dad was gambling and losing all their money sometimes. He would comb my hair and get me dressed and take me to the racetrack with him. He once said he lost money at the racetrack, but my mom found it and took it. She suspected he was giving the money to Mary. What could he say if he had lost it? Things were getting bad between my mom and dad. They were fighting and arguing a lot. Mary would call her at work and say, "I got your man." She moved us out after he refused to break things off with

Mary. He also would not marry Momma because she did not go to church. My grandfather was a preacher, so Dad needed a respectable church girl to take home. He eventually married Mary, but she gave him a life of misery and made it difficult for me to have a relationship with my father. I did not see my father after I was four until I was nineteen, even though he lived in a Chicago suburb.

BERNARD SR.

Cousin Dottie and her husband, Ronnie, introduced Momma to a guy named Bernard when things started getting bad between Momma and Dad. Mary wound up moving into the apartment after Momma, myself, and Auntie moved out. Momma only took her bed and refrigerator. She moved us into a one-bedroom apartment on 79th and Woodlawn. She had to work, so she allowed me to stay with Grandma in Robert Taylor Homes during the summer. Aunties DeDe and Melody took care of me when I was there. I went to kindergarten off 79th Street, and I would walk to school with another little girl.

Momma dated Bernard for a year. He wined and dined her, but there were issues before the marriage. My Auntie Melody told me he inappropriately touched her when she spent the night at our apartment and he was over there but my mom was away. Melody told Momma, but she still married him. When I brought it up to Momma, she said she had low self-esteem and did not think anyone would marry her because she had a child, so she went ahead with the marriage. It put a rift between her and Melody back then. I was very proud of Momma when she called and apologized to Melody when I reminded Momma about this incident. It made me proud of the power this book could have on the family and bringing darkness to light.

Momma married Bernard Wallace Sr. at city hall on April 20, 1980, with her best friend, Barbara, as her witness. Bernard said he did not want Momma's family to come over anymore. She knew right then she married a "nut job," as she put it. Cousin Dottie wanted to throw a reception, and he said no. He was controlling, and he was always accusing Momma of messing around. She got pregnant and worked the entire time at CNA. He was not working and made her pay all the bills. My brother was born on May 27, 1981. After she took my brother to get his shots, he had a fever and needed to rest. Bernard Sr. wanted to take the baby out to visit his brother, but my mother said no because of the fever. Bernard jumped on her back when she refused to let him take the baby, and she threw him off. I was six and scared. I tried to call Granddaddy on the phone. The police came, and they removed Bernard Sr. She started packing our things right away. She left him when my brother was only nine months old.

We went to live with my Auntie Debbie and her husband, Cecil. Everything was going well until he started doing drugs. Grandma was now taking care of my brother and me while my momma worked. Granddaddy took her back to get the rest of her things. He said to Bernard Sr., "You didn't know she could fight, huh?" Granddaddy was still a presence in our lives. Once again, we were in search of another place to live.

One of the elders on the Scaife family side, Madea, passed away, so we moved back to 65th place into her former apartment. Momma would have to get up so early and drop me off at my grandma's house. The early mornings were too hard on all of us, so for first and second grade, we would stay at Grandma's house on the weekdays and come home on the weekends. I attended Wadsworth Elementary behind my grandma's house from first to fifth grade. Grandma was handling most of my school affairs. I received acceptance into a high-achieving magnet school in fifth grade, but Grandma did not tell my mother the magnet school would pick me up at Wadsworth until it was past the deadline, so I missed that opportunity. One of my teachers told my mother to get me out of public school when I was in the fifth grade. She used the money she was saving for a new car and put my brother and me into St. Cyril, a Catholic school in Woodlawn not too far from our house.

My Grandma moved across the street from Wadsworth on Greenwood when I was in third grade. When the apartment across the hall from Grandma became available, we moved there. That move was good in that the family was together but mostly bad because there was a drug problem running through our family. My grandma was back on drugs. Auntie Robbin was dating a drug dealer and supplying drugs to the family, as I could tell, even from the eyes of a child. She would take me with her to his apartment. They had no idea I was paying attention to everything. When Grandma would have "people over," they would send all the kids (me, Devoy, Camilla, LaDena) to our apartment and tell us not to come across the hall. I can't say for certain if my mom was participating, but I was aware even at nine and ten that my family had a serious problem. We were not the only family. My entire neighborhood was suffering from an influx of crack into the community. It was a common occurrence to hear of someone overdosing and dying.

People were committing crimes against one another for drugs, so much that the community became largely unsafe. At sundown, you would see someone's mother and father looking like a zombie as they made their way to the closest crack house. Kids talked smack about one another and would use this to hurt each other. We were all going through this together. Many of my friends in the neighborhood did not have anyone to push them through school as a way out. The backlash was the tough-on-crime policies, and from the 1980s to the late 1990s, all the men in the community began to disappear into jails and prisons.

Twice, someone broke into our apartment. They came through the front door and the back door. Each time they only took money, and they knew exactly where it was. We called the police but there wasn't anything they could do. After the second break-in, Momma had enough, and she moved us a mile or so away to a third-floor apartment on 70th and Kimbark in "Pocket Town." We lived there until 1999, the year after I graduated from college. My brother Bernard, who was seventeen years old, had a new baby girl Melony (or Mel-Mel), with Tanya, his fifteen-year-old girlfriend. He was at a precarious age and had gotten arrested. My momma knew if she did not get him out of the city, he would end up like so many of his friends, dead or in jail. She transferred to CNA Insurance in Nashville, Tennessee, to escape the crime and hard life of Chicago.

MIGRATION TO NASHVILLE

Momma continued to work at CNA Insurance for four more years in Nashville before she retired. They all still live in Nashville, except Tanya, who moved back to Chicago when Melony was three. Melony was with her for a year or so before the unacceptable living conditions resulted in my brother going back to Chicago and bringing Melony to Nashville. My momma and brother raised Melony after that. She is doing great and is finishing college in 2022. My brother had three more daughters: the twins, Kaylyn and Jaylyn, are sixteen, and Robbin is thirteen. Bernard has done a great job raising his girls. I am proud of the man he has become, despite some of the things that have happened to him. I am also grateful to my mother for following a long tradition of migrating for a better life. Without her courage to leave the place she had always known, I am pretty sure my brother would not have made it to see his twenties and thirties and now forties. Tanya has done well for herself back in Chicago. She worked her way through school to become a nurse and had four more children.

This time of COVID-19 has been challenging for Momma. I went to visit her for Memorial Day 2021, and she did not look well at all. I heard prior to my visit she was falling. When I finally got a chance to sit with her, she told me she could not walk. I was in disbelief. My niece, Melony, and I helped her to her bed, and while helping her change clothes I saw her legs were swollen and red. I told her to please get checked out. I wanted to do more, but I needed to go home to Atlanta, where I had been living for twelve years with my husband and children. Two days later, she decided to check herself into the hospital. Doctors found her to have several issues going on.

For the next three months, I came back and forth from Atlanta to Nashville to manage her healthcare with my brother. We got her into a nursing home for rehabilitation. Things were going okay until they started to neglect her. This landed her back in the hospital. I went back for a week and sat with her at the hospital while we figured out the next step. That nursing home tried to convince me to return her there, and they would "treat her like a queen." She should have been treated like a queen from day one. We put her into another nursing home, where she stayed another month.

She went home in late August 2021. She is doing better and getting therapy at home. Her mobility has improved. Her relationship with my brother, Bernard, had a few bumps because of how she was speaking with him. I had to have a strong talk with Momma one day.

When I needed to have a real woman-to-woman talk with her, I said, "Shirley, I need to talk to you. I need you to resist becoming your mother. I know the pain you have gone through and wish your life could have been easier, but you are so strong. I know the last few months have been tough, and you don't feel in control of your life, but he is right there for you every day. He works hard every day for you and the girls. He is forty years old. Please do not treat him like a child. Please show respect for him. He needs you to respect him, or you will lose him. I know you do not want that."

She listened and thanked me for talking to her. The next day they had made up. I know it will continue to be difficult for her to fight past the pain, forgive her mother, and fight hard to overcome the results of the trauma. I did not like talking to my mother so strongly, but respectfully I needed to wake her up to her own situation. I had been coaching her through the nursing homes to be nicer to people. She sometimes has that frank way of speaking that all the women in the family have. I would just remind her they are there to help her. I saw her challenged in being dependent on others. It's easier to be mean to your own family than staff people who come in to help you. The three of us got closer through this health crisis of hers, and it would hurt to see their relationship break down at a time when I see the origins of so much of her pain and the beginning of her healing.

I told her she should be proud of who she is. She has overcome so much. She made a family out of friends with people like Barbara, Patricia, and Janice, who stayed friends through adulthood. Barbara passed away some years ago, though. She raised two children who are committed to raising up the next generation better than the last. She helped my brother raise four beautiful daughters, Melony, Kaylyn, Jaylyn, and Robbin. Prior to COVID-19, she would travel at least quarterly to Atlanta and stay with me and help care for her grandson, Muhammad, when I needed to travel for work and always for his birthday parties in December. Many times, she would stay here with my dad, Vernest, when he would visit from Arkansas, where he retired. It would warm my heart to see them become good friends again and come together for their grandson and me. She is a spitfire lady, and having the time and opportunity to document her life and our life is something I will treasure forever.

I love you, Momma!

PART 3

TIFFANY

CHAPTER 5

School Years

GROWING UP IN CHICAGO

My earliest memory from at least two years old is the movement of the city—the sounds of the cars, people's laughing, yelling, fighting, and music lofting from open windows and the street. The smell of food like barbecue and fried fish was always in the air as we moved through the city. My momma took my hand as we stepped onto a Chicago Transit Authority bus. I would investigate the faces on the bus, wondering who they were, how they lived, and where they were going. I always wondered why I had this sort of curiosity at such a young age. People would smile at me and mention how cute I was. They would come up and try to pinch my fat cheeks, saying, "You look like a Cabbage Patch Kid!"

My dad, Vernest Cantrell, grew up in Wynne, Arkansas, and moved to Chicago in the early 1970s to work as a porter on Amtrak. He worked there until he retired in 2008. He was a sweet man and had a twin, Earnest. He liked Momma because she was tough and cute. Unfortunately, even after they fell in love, he never wanted to marry her because she was not a church girl and because of what he saw from my grandma. My grandfather was a pastor. Mary was a church girl, and my dad thought she was more acceptable to become his wife. My dad was around when I was small, but when I was two, he chose Mary over my momma and me, married her, and had two kids. She would call Momma at her job and say, "I took your man." They were all in their mid-twenties and immature. Mary had forbidden my father from seeing me, and along with my momma's resolute independence, I did not see him again until I was nineteen. The decision to marry Mary was a regret of his because she was a mean and evil woman to him and everyone. He worked hard and provided a good life to Mary, my stepsister Nia, and stepbrother Lil' Vernest. He always felt guilty about allowing her to keep us apart for so long. He also never provided any support to my mother for my upbringing, which was another serious issue of contention between he and I when we reconnected when I became an adult.

Momma worked hard to take care of me and keep me in good daycare centers while working and seeking stable housing for us. When I was one year old, Grandma lost Aunt Daisy's house on 71st Street. She wanted my mother to move with her and the rest of my aunts to the Robert Taylor Homes, a housing development known as "the projects" on the South Side off 55th Street. My mother did not want to move me into that environment where gangs, drugs, and violence were present. She moved in with some family, but that environment was chaotic, and many nights she did not sleep before going to work. Momma named me after Tiffany & Co., the diamond company. Then she connected with a friend Ronnie who had a daughter named Tiffany.

My momma, me, Ronnie, and Big Tiff, as I always called her, shared a two-bedroom apartment.

I am the oldest child of my mother and the first grandchild of the family. I was an obedient child. I remember being two or three, and my momma would tell me to sit on the couch while she took a nap, and I would be sitting there until she woke up.

The next child born after me was my cousin Devoy. He and I were always two peas in a pod. He was a charismatic little boy whose smile would make you beam back at him. He was handsome, and over the years of our life he became my "brother-cuz," because cousin ("cuz") never quite encapsulated the love I had for him and how close we were.

When I was six, we moved back into the family building off Stony Island across from Jackson Park, which borders Lake Michigan. Most people know of the area now because President Barack Obama has built his Presidential Library there. I grew up in the same area as Michelle Obama, and the first Black President's Library is in the same park where I learned to dance and spent my childhood. The South Side brought me up with love for my culture and my people, which has carried me through my life.

When I was seven years old, Harold Washington became the first Black mayor of Chicago. He was always out in the community and on TV, speaking positively to Black children. I heard him. I believed I could do anything. Jessie Jackson also ran Rainbow Push out of Chicago, and you could not go anywhere or listen to the radio without hearing his slogan,

"If my mind can conceive it, if my heart can believe it, I know I can achieve it because I am somebody! Respect me! Protect me! Never neglect me! I am somebody!"

I loved the time I grew up in. It was before the internet and before children were exposed to so much, and everyone was not afraid of everything. I had a lot of freedom growing up to traverse the city.

THE SOUL VERSUS THE BODY

Living in our family apartment building was always fun and eventful. Someone was always cooking, visiting, or throwing a party. On the Fourth of July, when I was seven, we were grilling out in the backyard, and it started to storm. Somehow the back door became locked, and my older cousin, Darryl "Fujji," was told to go around through the front and unlock the back door. As his ever-faithful shadow, I set off to follow him. As he ran down the stairs, I was right behind him, but I was wearing my new white Dr. Scholl's sandals with wooden soles. Rain, stairs, and running in wood sandals were not a good combination. I slipped on the top stair, turned in midair, and hit the side of my head on the bottom concrete step. Everything went dark.

My next memory is watching my body lifted by my cousin Marcus "Bay." My entire family was there, surrounding me near the stairs on the first floor. I had split my head open, and it was gushing blood. Someone brought out a pink towel they wrapped around my head. They were all frantic as I lay there unconscious. Someone smacked my face, and they talked about whether to call an ambulance or take me to the hospital. They checked, and I was breathing. My momma was a nervous wreck and looked like she was going to pass out.

They decided to take me to the hospital since it was just down the street. No one knew how long it would take to wait on an ambulance in 1983 in the middle of the crack epidemic and gang warfare on the South Side of Chicago. As they started to move me, I was back in my body. Now I felt a pounding pain in my head. They changed the towel out and whisked me to the back seat of a car while my mother gently cradled my head. She looked so worried. Years later, I understood the significance of my memories of leaving my body and what it would mean to my spiritual development. Even at that young age, I had the clearest understanding of the difference between the soul and the physical body. I decided then to live through my soul and not my body.

BORED, BORED, BORED

My education was always a central character in my upbringing. I attended public school in Woodlawn at Wadsworth Elementary, which was between 64th and 65th and University. It was a huge building about as long as two city blocks. My grandmother lived behind it on 64th Street when I was in first through third grade. Then she moved on the other end of the block on 65th and Greenwood. I would stay with her during the week and go back to my momma's house off Stony Island on the weekends. Eventually, my mother moved into the apartment next door to my grandmother so we could be together all the time and be closer to the rest of the family. My Aunties Valerie and Debbie were living with Grandma or nearby. By the time I was ending fourth grade, Momma thought it was better to stay together and not have us with my grandma during the week because of Grandma's drug use and the people she had around. I wished we had just stayed in the family building off Stony Island, two blocks from St. Cyril, where my brother and I would soon be attending. There were other reasons why I wished we did not live in that building, which would ultimately lead to a move in another year when someone repeatedly broke into our apartment.

I had great teachers at Wadsworth. Ms. Clausen was my first-grade teacher. She had brown hair and was nice to me. Ms. Kilmartin was second grade, and Grandma signed all my report cards that year. I was showing some issues with self-control per the report card. Ms. Thomas was third grade, and I had Mrs. Smith for fourth. My momma bought Alex Haley's *Roots* when I was in the fourth grade, and I read it after she finished it. I enjoyed the story and was very curious about Black history, and this was one of the first novels I read with Black characters. I read it again in sixth grade and in high school. At a parent-teacher conference in fourth grade, Mrs. Smith told my mother: "Get her out of public school or it will swallow her up. Do what you have to do, but get her out." I tested and received acceptance at a magnet school across town, but Grandma never told my mother the school bus would pick me up from Wadsworth and take me to the magnet school. My mom had to find another way.

It took some doing and another year, but Momma took the $300 she was saving for a car and registered my brother and me for St. Cyril Catholic Elementary School and bought us uniforms. I started St. Cyril in the sixth grade. The church and rectory were midway between our house and the school.

St. Cyril was torn down in the mid-2000s.

St. Cyril was a small brick building that looked like a factory. Mr. Wozniak was the principal. He was a jovial Polish man with brown hair and a bit of a potbelly. He had been there for a long time when I started at St. Cyril. Ms. Jacobsen was my new sixth-grade teacher. She was a thin young White lady with blond hair. She was nice, and I think it was her first year when I started. I liked St. Cyril. It was a challenge academically for all of a month. Then I became bored and disruptive with the self-control issues showing up again. I blamed the school for not challenging me enough after hearing my mother discuss this with the school. I would finish everything they gave me and then distract the other students who might not have their work completed. After a discussion with Momma, Mr. Wozniak decided to have me work in the school office while the secretary went to lunch. This was a sheer act of grace on his part for me. I learned great organization skills, how to type, answer the phone appropriately, how to write a letter, how to greet people, and more. I learned and excelled working in the office in sixth, seventh, and eighth grade.

I loved my seventh-grade teacher, Ms. Peaches. She was a tall African American woman with a short mushroom hairstyle. She did not have any eyebrows and would draw them on with black eyeliner in an upside-down V shape, making her look like a Vulcan from Star Trek. She was a tough yet caring teacher, and she pushed me hard. But, again, in my monotony of worksheets and memorization, I had an idea. We had desks with lift lids, so we would tape mirrors to primp from the inside. You could also talk to the person next to you as you pretended to get out your books.

One day, I borrowed a black eyeliner pencil from one of the other girls. When Ms. Peaches left the room, I lifted my desk lid and went about drawing my Vulcan eyebrows. I passed the eyeliner around, and the rest of the girls drew their Vulcan eyebrows on as well. Ms. Peaches came back into the classroom and started teaching. We were all coming unglued and giggling, waiting on her to notice. That triggered her to stop and give us that stare of death, and when she did, she saw the eyebrows.

"What is going on here?" asked Ms. Peaches.

Before anyone could say anything, someone yelled out, "It was Tiffany Green. She passed around the eyeliner, Ms. Peaches."

I raised my desktop up and tried to wipe off my Vulcan brows, but the cheap eyeliner just turned into a black smudge all over the top of my face.

"Tiffany, get up right now and see me in the hallway," demanded Ms. Peaches.

I said, "Yes, ma'am," hanging my head and glaring at the girl who tricked on me.

I went into the hall and waited for Ms. Peaches. She took a long time to come outside. I could hear her reprimanding the class and saying how disappointed she was in them. Then she came out to deal with me. I just knew I was going to get suspended. Momma would definitely put me on punishment for this.

"Miss Green!"

"Yes, Ms. Peaches?"

"What's going on with you?"

"I don't know. I was just bored," I whined.

"Come on now. You cannot keep using that as an excuse. I know you are a smart girl, but I was only gone for five minutes. And you got all the girls wrapped up in your shenanigans."

I made the excuse, "But they did not have to do it."

She replied, "You are right, but you are the leader in there. Do you understand? I need you to be more responsible. It hurt my feelings, but I know you were just trying to be funny. And it worked, because the class thought it was very funny."

I was embarrassed now, so I apologized. "I am really sorry, Ms. Peaches. I won't do anything like that again. I will go tell Mr. Woz."

She looked down on me on said, "Girl, I didn't say all that. We are going to move on this time. Go clean your face and come back in, sit down, and don't tell anyone about our conversation. Let the class think you got in more trouble. Okay?"

"Yes, ma'am." I grinned, then I dropped my smile, hung my head, and walked to the bathroom, then returned to class. I flung down into my seat with all the dramatics like I was in big trouble.

When I was in college, I came back to the school to visit Ms. Peaches right before she retired, and we had the biggest laugh about that whole situation. She did so much for my confidence, and she made me believe in myself. I didn't have many Black teachers after St. Cyril, so she and Ms. Duncan, the eighth-grade teacher, were big inspirations to me and all the students who stay in touch on social media. Academically, I received the A honor roll every quarter from sixth grade through eighth grade. When I came back to visit the school during college, they told me no one had beat my record for A honor rolls. Eventually, the city demolished the school building and church.

LINK UNLIMITED

A few months into eighth grade, Mr. Wozniak called me to his office. He had a stern look on his face, which was off-putting. I had to think if I had done something. I had straightened up my shenanigans as I was preparing for high school. I planned to attend Whitney Young, a high-achieving public school in the south loop if I got accepted through their application process, or Kenwood, a good public high school in Hyde Park that had great programs for high-achieving students. He put some papers in front of me and told me to fill them out. I gave him a confused look.

He said, "I spoke to Mom, and she is aware and is okay with this."

I was puzzled but intrigued they were conspiring about me. Momma usually tells me everything. It was an application for some program called Link Unlimited. I had no way of knowing these papers would change the course of my education and life. I answered the questions to the best of my ability over about two hours.

He took the packet without even cracking a smile, which was unlike him. He told me he had arranged with Mom to drop me off at the house since it was late. We left promptly, and he drove me a little over a mile to my building at 70th and Kimbark. It was October, so it was dark at 5:00 p.m. I asked on the ride over what was next, and he said, "I'll let you know." I did not ask much about it after that. I had learned during those almost three years of working in the office that Mr. Woz was a straight shooter. His reluctance to tell me anything about this program was his way of protecting me from disappointment. Why get me excited about going to a great school or the funds needed until we "got to the bridge"?

Two weeks later, my mother said we had to attend a meeting about the papers I filled out. We went to St. Dorothy Catholic Church one evening on the bus. We got there early and sat and watched as family after family piled into the gym. I started meeting people and found out there were kids from all over the city. Many of them looked well-off from the way they dressed. The Link staff started the program, and the first thing they discussed was the selection process and the income restrictions. I thought many of these kids looked too well-off to be applying for a scholarship program for low-income students. Now I was nervous and intimidated. Did I have the grades and the volunteer work to be competitive with kids from Catholic schools throughout Chicago to attend a top private high school? There were tables with staff from all the best schools in Chicago with their application packets. I walked around and talked to St. Ignatius, which was coed, and Mother McCauley, an all-girls school. During the meeting, Link told us if they selected us for an interview with them, we would hear in January. This was November—a week or so before Thanksgiving. The application was due in early December.

Once I decided I wanted to attend a Catholic school, I couldn't wait to tell Mr. Woz—and fix my application. The minute I saw him, I said, "Where is that application I filled out? Please don't tell me you sent it in already."

With a coy smile, he said, "No way. It's been right here on my desk waiting on you to understand what it was."

I wanted to work on it more and really perfect my responses now that I understood the program was looking for scholars who had the potential for personal leadership, achievement, and success, both in and out of school. Most exciting, the program matched you with a donor family who would give financial and personal support. That changed the trajectory of my future. Link has been around for over fifty years and continues to make an impact for students across Chicago. One day, I hope to sponsor a Link student, perhaps with some of the proceeds from this book.

I took the application home over the weekend. I wrote and rewrote the responses. I decided to ask Mr. Chaney to review them with me. Mr. Chaney was a retired school administrator who volunteered at the school and had connections to my family for over twenty years. He lived two doors down from the family building off Stony Island, so I had seen him over the years, but I did not get to know him well until I attended St. Cyril. He took an interest in me because of my academic skills and his connections to my family.

I loved listening to his stories about the civil rights movement and how he picketed and worked to increase equity for Black students and teachers in Chicago Public Schools. He had lung cancer but did not tell me until a few months before then. By the time he told me, he was very ill, so every Saturday that I was free, I would go over to his house and sit with him. Sometimes I would clean up his room. He was still smoking, so there was a lot of me fussing at him. He imparted so much wisdom on me for those hours on those Saturdays. He was like a grandfather to me by then. I let him read the application. He gave his perspective on what they were really looking for, which was authenticity. He told me always to be myself and that I was enough. He encouraged me to apply to St. Ignatius because it was the oldest school in Chicago and had the best college preparation. It was also near downtown, and he knew how much I loved going downtown to window shop.

Mr. Chaney passed away that next spring. I was sad but grateful for the time with him. He had prepared me for his passing, and I attended his service. Before he transitioned, we celebrated my getting an interview and acceptance into Link Unlimited and St. Ignatius. He was truly one of my angels, one of many people who schooled me at school and in the community. I graduated from St. Cyril as the Valedictorian with the help of Mr. Chaney, Ms. Peaches, Mr. Woz, and Momma. I must give a special shout-out to the Men's Club at St. Cyril Church, who donated the $435 for my registration to St. Ignatius. It was something that could have prevented me from attending.

DABBLING IN THE NATION

Pocket town, where I lived on 70th and Kimbark, was near Nation of Islam (NOI) Mosque Maryam on 73rd and Stony Island. Although my great-great-Aunt Daisy died in 1969, her presence and particularly her leadership in the NOI also affected my youth. I grew up hearing stories about her house, how she cooked for Elijah Muhammad and other dignitaries there, and her and my Uncle Henry's leadership in the NOI. People would share stories about her famous bean pie while around the dinner table. Yes, the very same ones sold on corners in urban cities around the country. My mother would tell me stories about Ramadan and how Aunt Daisy would cook huge meals for the iftars (meal breaking daily fast at sunset). And she would tell me about going to the Temple. Aunt Daisy would have her come to her house and change into modest clothes and take her to the Temple. That Muslim influence always stayed with my mother and aunts, but none of them continued to be Muslim as they grew up.

Most importantly, I always had a relationship with God ever since my out of body experience at seven. I started to explore the Nation of Islam and going to the mosque when I was a teenager because it was a few blocks from our house. I was going down a difficult path from bad boyfriends and being sexually active way too young. I was seeking stability and more of a spiritual community. I would listen to Farrakhan on the radio, and one Savior's Day I decided to go to the mosque. I even wore a hijab, albeit it barely would stay on. I was a nervous wreck that day as I stood in the sister's line and went through a pat down to get inside. I walked inside with my mouth hanging open. It was such a beautiful site to see all the sisters in their white khimars "headscarves" pulled over their ears and pinned behind their head with fabric flowing down their back. I was directed to a seat in the back behind all the sisters. I listened intensely to the various speakers before Farrakhan spoke. I was there all day. I longed to be part of that community and started coming back often. I told my mother of my interest, and she was okay with it, so I took classes on Saturdays. To join the Nation, you had to write a perfect handwritten letter proclaiming you have heard the teachings of Elijah Muhammad and that "I bear witness there is no God but Allah and Muhammad is his servant and last apostle."

When Spike Lee's *Malcolm X* movie came out, I was wearing a hijab every day—even to school. Everyone was asking me about it at school. It was an emotional movie for me because I was dabbling in the Nation. I connected my own family history and how Denzel Washington portrayed Malcolm X. I had read the autobiography of Malcolm X by then, so I was very familiar with his story. I moved around alone most of the time because my mother was single, and I had to be very independent. Men often approached me, which made me uncomfortable. I loved the environment of the mosque because it appeared wholesome. I turned in my letter, but I ultimately left the Nation of Islam shortly after because a guy tried to court me, which scared me away. I was only sixteen and did not know anyone to confide in about that. I wished I had stuck with it, but it was not my time.

I became more impacted by the trappings of the street into a double life. I fell into a bad crowd looking for a father figure. I was so young and impressionable. I wished my father had been around. I used to drink and smoke when I was with my friends, but I made sure my grades stayed on point since they were my ticket out of Chicago. My mother relied on me to do the right thing, and she gave me a lot of freedom, which I did abuse. I did my dirt, but it was God's grace that kept me safe through some hairy incidents in my teenage years on the streets of Chicago.

GROWING UP FAST

I came up during the crack epidemic. I can recall the first whispering of adults on our block when there were shootings over drugs. There was before crack and after crack. Before crack, we could play outside until it got dark and still stay out front if an older cousin was there. There were at least thirty kids on my block, from toddlers to teens, who looked after us younger kids. But after crack hit, mothers wanted us in their sight always, and when the streetlights started to flicker, you had to be in the house.

The city can teach you all sorts of things, good and bad. I had to learn to be independent as a girl and the oldest grandchild. The streets were not always nice to a girl child. You had to walk with a sense of owning the streets and knowing where you were. If you looked scared, you would likely become the victim of a crime.

My mother moved us to Greenwood in the apartment across from my grandma when I was in the third grade, and it was good for a little while until I began to see the things I had not seen when I left on the weekends. I saw firsthand the effects of drugs on everyone and especially my grandma and some of my aunts. Now in the building every day, I saw my grandma would have lots of friends over on Friday nights, and she would tell all the kids to stay at our house. I was nosy, so I wanted to know what was going on. Once when my grandma left, I snooped through her dresser trying to find out why she kept her room closed off. She had a tall dresser, and the bottom drawer had a sliding wood top, and she kept private things in there. It was there I found a plate, razors, two pipes, a lighter, and a few spoons burned on the bottom with specks of brown residue that looked like burned plastic. I did not know what it was exactly, but I knew it was drugs. I was eight or nine years old then. I placed everything back and left her room.

I felt anxious all the time that Grandma would die doing drugs. It also made me more nervous being around her. This was a constant concern that eventually came to reality in 1992 when I was sixteen. Until now, I felt ashamed of the sense of relief I witnessed from the adults in the family when she passed. Her addiction showed on her tiny frame. As a child, I saw things one way, and my memory may be clouded or distorted, but she was in a better place, and we didn't have to worry anymore about her. I hope she is looking over me and proud of me for attempting to tell a fuller story of her life.

I got top grades and was very outgoing academically, and I loved performing. I danced at the Jackson Park field house and at talent shows in the community throughout my childhood. I sang, did tap and jazz dance, rapped, and was a cheerleader. Sometimes all this excellence made me an outsider in the neighborhood as girls would say I "talked White" or wanted to be White because I focused on excelling. I mainly played with my cousins, but there were a few girls I played with from the neighborhood, including Anisha, who lived on Greenwood. She was a few years older than me and very protective of me because she was the oldest and had three little brothers. I only met her mother once or twice when she answered the door when I asked if Anisha could come out to play. Her mother was beautiful, and she looked just like her. Her boyfriend murdered her while Anisha and her brothers slept upstairs. Anisha was twelve or thirteen then. Her Aunt Ruth, who had moved into their home, raised her and her brothers. She stays in Chicago and is married to Alfred. They have been together for over twenty years. I was in their wedding party. They have one daughter, Fallon, who is my goddaughter. Anisha and I helped each other grow up and navigate the tough streets of Chicago.

Performing in 1989 at St. Cyril Church talent show with friends Erica and Sherise reenacting *School Daze,* "I don't want to be alone tonight."

I can see how my father not being in my life until adulthood made me do things I probably would not have done if he were around. The first "crush" I remember was a Hispanic boy named Benjamin Santana, who was in my third and fourth-grade class. He had the cutest mushroom haircut and was always sweet to me. He and his older brother, Abraham, were the only non-Black students at Wadsworth. I had boyfriends starting at age thirteen, and looking back, I was seeking a father figure. I needed direction and acceptance from those young men until I was in my late twenties. I had to learn how to love myself. Without a father, that process took time, effort, and investment in myself. I am grateful I got there without having babies too young, which would have slowed my personal growth.

When you grow up in a large city, you learn to walk and behave to put on a front that you don't want to be bothered. I had to do this using public transportation and walking in the neighborhood. I had to take three buses or two buses and a train to get to St. Ignatius. My mother worked at CNA Insurance downtown for twenty-three years, and for those four years I was in high school, we rode together most mornings. One morning I had a scary incident. In the dead of winter, she did not go with me. I was either leaving out early to study or she had something else to do that day. It was dark as I walked one block south to 71st Street and crossed to wait for the bus to take me east to Jeffrey to catch the express bus downtown.

On 71st Street, there was a viaduct to my right or east, and to my left or west I could see all the way to Cottage Grove to watch for the bus. Since it was dark, I was on high alert. I was looking east through the viaduct and west for the bus. I saw a guy walking west on the other side of the viaduct. I then looked for the bus, not wanting any interaction.

After too long a time, I realized he had not passed me, so I looked back east. I didn't see him at first, but after staring there for a few moments, I saw him peek at me from behind one of the arches. I did not dare take my eyes off him. That was looking like a victim and asking for an assault. I stood my ground and dropped my heavy book bag off my shoulder onto the ground with a thud. I was letting him know not to fuck with me. Right as I dropped the bag, the bus eased up on the side of me. I was so relieved.

The bus driver let me on, and he saw the guy and asked whether I knew him. I said, "No, sir," so I stood near the driver who drove slowly through the viaduct. When we passed the guy, the bus driver pointed at him as to say, "Leave this girl alone." That was a close one.

One night, I was hanging out with a boyfriend named Terry. He was cute and looked like a young Tupac from "Brenda's got a baby." I was the girl all my boyfriend's friends thought was cool. I met him after my time at the Nation. We were all hanging out one night, drinking. I was sitting in his car, and I had on a hoodie. I was drunk. A car of guys came around the corner once, then circled again. Terry and his boys saw this and went and got their guns. They instructed me to stay in the car, which I did. Now I was scared. I wanted to leave, but I was too drunk to drive home. It was tense for a moment as each group of guys sized each other up, and Terry asked them if they were looking for someone.

They were there to buy weed on a tip from someone they knew in common. Terry told them no one had anything. This was a lie, but you did not sell to anyone you did not know. They could have been undercover police. Another tell was when they saw me sitting in the car and asked who I was. I had the hoodie over my head, so they could not tell if I was a girl or boy. Terry let them know I was his girlfriend. They left after that. Terry told me to go home. I was still drunk, but it was time to go. I got home about twenty minutes later because I was driving so slowly.

I lived that double life well. In the Link Unlimited program, it was required we attend teen mass at St. Dorothy Catholic Church once a month. Link had a hundred students, but teen mass attracted them and their friends. We also had to attend overnight religious retreats annually. It was at the Christ and Others retreat I connected with a young man named Oliver. He and I would date the rest of our sophomore year to senior year of high school. He was wholesome and handsome with dark black hair and green eyes. We were very much in love in high school. We went to prom together, and the entire family came over to see me off. But it was his prom. I did not go to St. Ignatius's prom. Oliver and I parted ways in early July before college.

COLLEGE DECISIONS

I flew out to tour a few colleges in the fall before graduation. I visited Williams College in October 1993, which was in upstate Massachusetts. It was a picturesque campus tucked in a valley on the edge of Massachusetts, Vermont, and New York. It was Halloween weekend, and the campus was a plethora of fall oranges, reds, and brown in the trees. It was cool outside but not too cold. I was toured around on the first day by my host. I remember seeing rugby for the first time there. The travel to Williams was a concern. I flew into Schenectady, New York, and then caught a taxi for a ninety-minute drive into Massachusetts through harrowing tree-lined hilly streets to the campus. I was at once concerned about the feasibility of traveling there in the winter with snow and how I would afford to get back and forth to Chicago.

Vanderbilt flew all the Black student applicants into Nashville for what they called "Black Student Weekend" in early December 1993. They made the campus feel like there were hundreds of Black students. I learned later most of them were from Tennessee State University and Fisk University, two miles from the campus. Nashville seemed like a great city to me. It was not too big or small, it was clean, and there were a ton of colleges, history, and Black culture.

The university escorted us in groups of ten with a few Black upperclassmen to tell anecdotal stories about the campus and all the great things about Vanderbilt and Nashville. The tour ended with a catered reception and lunch. It was fancy, but I was not too nervous after spending four years in the upscale school environment of St. Ignatius. At the end of the luncheon, the president spoke and made his pitch for why we should choose Vanderbilt. Then he surprised us and said, "We have already accepted you all into the class of 1998."

Everyone was stunned initially and not sure what he was saying. With a bit more reassurance, we all began to clap. The admissions team gave us our acceptance letters and let us know they mailed copies home simultaneously. I was so excited and proud that "I did it." Vanderbilt was easier to get to than Williams, and I really wanted to be in the South.

During the visit, I spent time in the Black Cultural Center, a.k.a. "the House." It was a little Black mecca in the middle of campus. There was a living room, a computer lab, a kitchen, and a few meeting rooms. You could meet people there, and it was more comfortable for me because it was full of Black students versus sitting in the dining hall full of White students right across the walkway from the house.

I also applied to Florida A&M University and four other schools using the Common Application. The decision was going to be tough. I turned to mentors from the Link program for help.

One of my mentors was Roseanne Swain. She was the wife of John Swain, a Link alum, attorney, and sister-in-law to Jonathon Swain, another alum who attended St. Ignatius during the time I was there. Roseanne was a former Pepsi executive who met John through business, fell in love, and moved to Chicago after they married. She and I got to know one another during the Christ and Others retreat. I remember not liking her at first because she was too bubbly. She went out of her way to model for me how to be professional even when you did not get along with someone. Eventually, I warmed up to her.

When it was time to choose a college, she and John made an incredible brunch for me at their apartment. Dr. Julie Welborn, who also worked for Link and had become a special person to me, attended the brunch. John and Roseanne presented me with a gift. It was a Bible with my name and "Woman of God" in gold on the front. I treasure that Bible and still have it. We ate, laughed, and talked about the school visits and how life was about to change. I was still undecided and all over the place. They were instrumental in helping me lay out the pros and cons of each school and what factors to consider. We looked at the cost of getting back and forth to school from Chicago and thoroughly looked at all the financial aid packages. As a first-generation college student, no one in my immediate Green/Boyd family had attended college, so their advice helped me to make the right choice. I chose Vanderbilt over Williams and Florida A&M University after long and careful consultation and consideration with them. The bonus was my cousin Darryl was a student there in his junior year when I would start in the fall. Vanderbilt also gave me the best financial aid package.

I tried to live it up the rest of my summer in Chicago before moving to Nashville. Oliver and I broke up to give each other the space we needed, or rather, *he* needed before college. He would go on to Florida A&M University. I was staying downtown most of the time with my best friend, Vikki. She was in school at Columbia College. We had a great time, going to parties and just being young and free in the city. At one of the parties, I met a friend of a friend of hers. He was a very handsome young man with long locks. We were friendly at the party and really attracted to one another. We talked on the phone three times and decided to get together.

My momma and brother were going to stay overnight at Cousin Dottie's house, so I would have the house to myself. She told me not to have anyone over while she was gone. I disobeyed her and invited him over late on a Friday night. We talked and watched TV. He kept trying to do more than I was ready to do. He would stop and then start back up. I told him I did not know him like that and was not interested in having sex. He told me he understood and there were other things he could do. I relented and allowed him to perform oral sex, but he did not stop.

In the heat of the moment, he entered me, and I started to scream and push him off. I told him I did not want that. He behaved as though one act made it okay to do the other act. It did not. I was scared now and told him to leave my house. It was about 4:00 a.m., and he said the buses were not running, so he would leave when the sun came up. I locked myself in my bedroom and pushed the bed against the door. I cried and was angry at myself for disobeying my mother. It was two weeks before I was to leave for Nashville. Should I call the police? Should I tell my mother? Would this prevent me from going to college? I had worked so hard to get there. When the sun came up, I heard the front door open and close. I waited a while and came out of my room. He was gone.

Growing up in Chicago made me mature beyond my years, and I was so close to my move. But the city had other ideas and left me bruised on my way out. The rape and drug addiction in my family had me ready for a change. I committed to living right and staying focused on my academics. One decision and my life could go down the wrong road. I only told Vikki what happened. I did not tell my mother until I was in my thirties. I did not call the police. I left the pain of that night in Chicago and moved on as best I could with my life into college.

CHAPTER 6

Nashville

FACING MY FEARS

I did everything I could to suppress the worry and occasional nightmares about "the incident." I was fearful telling anyone could jeopardize my move. I worked so hard through Link Unlimited and St. Ignatius College Prep. Now, I was on my way as the first college student in my family. I would not let anything or anyone stop me now.

One of the last social events was at Vikki's and her roommate Val's apartment. She had many friends, but it was a small gathering for an end of the summer get-together. We were having a great time, and then *he* showed up. I initially did not recognize him because he had cut off the beautiful shoulder-length locks that had attracted me to him. It was only when everyone began asking him about his locks I realized it was him. I was so afraid I began to hyperventilate. I didn't know what to do, so I ran into the bathroom.

Vikki followed me in and tried to console me. She asked me what was going on. I tried to tell her through my crying what had occurred a week ago with him. For him to show up with all his hair cut off was a clear sign he was worried the police would be looking for him.

"Oh my god, Tiffany," Vikki said, hugging me close. "We need to call the police."

"No! No!" I stressed. "I can't deal with this. I leave for college in four days. My mother will be so disappointed. This will mess up everything, and I won't let it. No, I just want to move on and leave Chicago."

"Son of a bitch. He's got some nerve showing up. What the fuck?" Vikki was livid. "He just can't get away with this," she said, still trying to convince me. But I wouldn't relent. "Well, he has to go then," she said as she left the bathroom. I heard a commotion as she confronted him about assaulting me.

"You hurt my girl? Motherfucker, are you crazy? You got to get the hell out of here," Vikki shouted from the other room.

I could hear him making excuses and asking to speak to me when she said, "No, just leave."

I was peeping from the bathroom and saw everyone was confused. But Vikki would not snap on a friend about another friend unless it was serious, so they did not ask questions. The guys told him to leave and walked him out. Vikki asked everyone else there to leave so we could have privacy. It was just Vikki, Val, and me left. It took me time to gather myself. I cried some more, but when I left her apartment, I did not cry about the sexual assault again. It was four days and counting until I left for Vanderbilt University.

It took me years to come to terms with what occurred and say out loud I was raped. I felt guilty because I disobeyed my mother and had male company. I know now it was not my fault—no means no—but it took therapy to understand why I needed validation from men to feel good about myself. Every girl I knew growing up was having sex, and I had been having sex from my early teens. I also knew the girls I grew up with dealt with assault at least once as a teenager or younger. The pervasiveness of molestation and sexual abuse was too commonplace and was why I ultimately did not feel confident if I had told someone I would have been believed and protected. It was certainly a misguided thought, but I did the best I could. My focus was on my future.

RETURNING TO THE SOUTH

My mother asked everyone in the family to drive us to Nashville, but no one was available. My Auntie Robbin's boyfriend, James, was available, but he had something to do in two days, so my mother and he would have to take me and turn right back around to Chicago. We filled his Cadillac to the brim. I had to squeeze myself into the car for the eight-hour drive from Chicago to Nashville. I slept most of the ride and felt butterflies thinking about what I had just endured and the unknown of this new place.

My dream of college was finally coming true. I was out of Chicago and free. I made the migration back to the South almost sixty years after Aunt Daisy left Alabama. I wonder, was she as nervous as I was?

My mother was reading the directions from the map sent with my dorm information. We got off the highway downtown, but it was nothing compared to Chicago. There were eight and twelve-story buildings toward campus. Right across from my dorm was a huge Loews hotel and a Pizza Hut on the other corner. When we arrived, the beauty of the campus and all the flowers struck me. I didn't remember seeing so many flowers the first time, maybe because it was December. We found Kissam Quad, and the volunteer students called vuceptors checked me into my single room, unloaded the car, and delivered it all to my dorm room. That was a relief for my mother and me.

With the car unloaded, Momma and James found a nearby hotel where he could sleep for four hours. She came back in his car and then went up to my room to unpack. There were all the necessities: bedding, toiletries, plastic bins, a record player, and a tape deck. I had Brandy's "I Wanna Be Down" on tape and played it while we set up my room. We made a customary Target run for snacks before buying my textbooks and grabbing lunch. Together we chatted about the first day of classes and how not to get lost.

On the walk back to the dorm, my momma told me how she and everyone in the family were proud of me. I was smiling, but inside I was sad thinking about this being the last time I would be with my momma for months. I was also pushing down anguish about the assault and wanting to tell my mother and be consoled by her but also not wanting to spoil this occasion. She deserved this peace of mind that her daughter had made it to college. It was her success too.

We arranged my books on the shelf above the desk and sat silently on the bed. Then I hugged her so hard. I did not want her to go. I walked her to the Cadillac and hugged her again. I could see she was holding back tears, and so was I.

"Be good and take care of yourself," she said. Then I watched the Cadillac drive off.

TIME TO FIND MY PEEPS

I stood there in the parking lot for what seemed like forever, but it was only two minutes.

"Okay, Tiffany," I said to myself. "Now what?"

I went back to my room and got dressed in my cutest outfit. I was looking for my people. I had only seen one other Black girl on my floor. She was unpacking with her whole family, so we only said hello. I was on the edge of campus, so I set out for the Black Cultural Center. It was 3:00 p.m., so I had an hour before meeting my cousin Darryl "Fujji." He was living off campus, but he told me to come to the Carmichael Tower dorms by 4:00 p.m. to meet him. I found the Black Cultural Center, but there was no one in there. I looked around again and then walked back toward West End Avenue. The towers looked just like Chicago housing projects. They were two on one block and two across the street.

When I walked toward the entrance, I could see six to eight Black guys standing outside. I was nervous as I approached but was so grateful to see my cousin Fujji apart of the group. He gave me a big hug and begrudgingly said, "Well, let me introduce you to my teammates." He was in his third year as a football player. "Hey, this is my cousin Tiffany. Look out for her, but don't fuck with her."

The guys nodded their heads in a sort of knowing way. He introduced me to Royce, Ronnie, Robert, the twins, and this guy called Tank. I hung out with my cousin and the teammates in the lounge inside the dorm. Eventually, Fujji left, and I continued hanging out there with mainly Royce and Tank. Tank began flirting with me right after my cousin left. I reciprocated, and after that day, we began a long-term relationship that lasted for seven years. Tank was a football player for Vanderbilt, but he got caught smoking weed, and they kicked him off the team a year later. He spent a year at Florida A&M University but still never made it to the NFL. We had a lot of love for one another. He was a good guy but lost his way for a time after getting kicked out of school and not making it into the league. We lived together for three years, and he encouraged my entrepreneurial side. Ultimately, we parted ways about three years after I graduated from college.

The rest of my first year was jam-packed with developing new friendships, trying to stay on top of my classes, and working. I had to work to have money. I did not want to be a burden on Momma. I qualified for Federal Work-Study, which provides part-time jobs for undergraduates with financial needs. The program encourages work related to the student's course of study. I worked in the computer lab, which began my experience in technology-related industries, which would continue throughout my career.

My classes were challenging. I took Drama (B-); Human Sexuality (B), which was a hundred-plus person class all my friends took, and it was fun; and Elementary Spanish (C+), which I thought I would do better in. Then I failed Analytic Geometry and Calc 1. I ended my first semester with a 2.6 GPA. That sucked. I thought I would do better. I had to be more strategic in choosing my classes. Working and classes continued to be a balancing act throughout college.

Life was simple until October when I got a call. My cousin, Devoy, had a gunshot wound in the back from a drive-by shooting. He would be paralyzed from the waist down. I did not get to see him again until Christmas break.

HEATWAVE OF 1995 IN CHICAGO

I finished out my first year of college successfully and went back to Chicago for the summer. I was in Inroads, an internship and leadership program. I worked at GE Capital the summer before college, and they asked me back for another summer. I moved back in with Momma and my brother. I commuted every day from the South Side to the Chicago suburbs on the Metra train. The job was decent. I was working with other teens from Inroads, but the corporate environment was not for me. I was not excited to work there, and I guess it was apparent. They did not ask me back after that summer.

In July, it got so hot there were blackouts throughout the city. In one week, 739 people died from the heat. Most of them were elderly and African American. One steamy night, Anisha, Vikki, and I went out, and we were driving down Stony Island, past a funeral home. They were unloading bodies from a hearse, and the cover blew off, and we saw the tag on the foot of a corpse. There were so many people dying that cooling trucks were put in parking lots at funeral homes throughout the city but particularly on the South Side, where many of the poor Black people who died lived. It was a sad time. Those people did not have to die if the city had done a better job creating cooling stations and going from building to building in certain communities to check on the elderly. We lived on the third floor with no air conditioning. To sleep, I had to soak a sheet in cold water, wrap it around me, and lay in front of the fan in the window. The last part of the summer was miserable, and I was ready to go back to Nashville.

Being back in Chicago also reminded me why I was so ready to leave. The crime, drugs, and poverty were inescapable, no matter where I worked. In Nashville, I had peace of mind and felt safe. I never came back to Chicago for a full summer after that. I permanently moved to Nashville.

My sophomore year, I moved into Cole Hall, an all-girl dorm in the center of campus. I had a single room again. Latrice and Kimberly were two years ahead of me and lived there as well as another good friend, Allison, who was the same year as me. All three of them were from Atlanta. In the spring of 1995, Latrice and Kimberly invited me to Atlanta for Freaknik, which was this annual spring break festival. It began in 1983 as a small picnic, and historically Black college students attended. By 1995, there were multiple parties, concerts, basketball games, and dance contests. It was a crazy few days as

350,000 people attended. The attendees shut down the city. We sat on I-285 for four hours in wall-to-wall traffic. People got out of their cars and danced in the street. The White people looked so nervous. Police just left everyone alone if they were not too rowdy. We went to parties but mostly drove around Atlanta and flirted with guys.

Unfortunately, in 1996 the mayor of Atlanta, Bill Campbell, under pressure from White citizens and business associations, made the event difficult with roadblocks and pushed the event to Memorial Drive in DeKalb County. By 1999, Freaknik died down due to heavy police presence, making it impossible to party.

BLACKTREE ENTERTAINMENT

Throughout those years, I was more than a typical college student. I was also an entrepreneur. My male best friend in college was a guy, also from Atlanta, named Jamaal Finkley. Jamaal and I started a company called BlackTree Entertainment, known today as BlackTree Media, the most viewed Black portal on YouTube.

We threw parties in Nashville as well as doing artist development and management with Tank and Felabi, another student athlete from New York. We threw the official after-party for the Budweiser Superfest, which was a concert of multiple hip-hop and R&B artists, in 1997. My brother, Bernard, was sixteen and was visiting me. I let him hang out with me. I was the vice president of BlackTree and the most responsible one among us to drive the rental van, so they decided I would pick up Wu-Tang from their hotel, get them to the club on time, and make sure they get back to the hotel after the party. This was right after the release of their *Wu-Tang Forever* album, so Wu-Tang was huge, and their heads were even bigger. This task was like wrangling cats—especially managing Method Man. He was outside of the hotel throwing rocks at the hotel signs, and all the White people were staring because they didn't know who he was. I was trying to get him to stop, but he was Method Man, a huge hip-hop star, and I was just a young lady who was driving him around.

He eventually stopped, and I got him, Raekwon, U-God, Ol' Dirty Bastard, Cappadonna, Masta Killa, Inspectah Deck, Ghostface Killah, and GZA in a van and drove them to the club where my company threw the biggest party Nashville had ever seen. My brother was witness. When we got there, I gave Bernard one instruction: "Do not mix your drinks." He did not listen, and before the night was over, he was outside vomiting. My brother and I still laugh at that story. He says, "I should have listened to you." That night was crazy and incredible. I got all of Wu-Tang back in the van, took them to Waffle House, and then dropped them back at their hotel.

GRADUATION AND STAYING IN NASHVILLE

I graduated in May 1998 from Vanderbilt with a degree in economics. I remember that day being crazy because I was running late trying to get all the family together to the right place on campus. Momma was there, and Auntie Melody, Auntie DeDe, Cousin Camilla and her daughter Jasmine, Cousin Devoy, and Granddaddy Jesse came. I was the first person in our family to graduate from college, and it was great to be surrounded by the love of the family. They came together for me, and I was so appreciative. No matter the struggles we face together, we still celebrate and lift each other up.

After graduating, I worked two jobs before finding my way. First, there was Mrs. Weiners Chicken, but getting up at 3:00 a.m. to make biscuits was too exhausting. Then I moved into technology, getting a job at CompUSA as a salesperson, something I had a real knack for as a natural people-person. It was there I was able to take computer training courses.

I honed my business skills during those years I was involved with BlackTree. Jamaal eventually got into legal trouble and dropped out of sight for years before resurfacing in Hollywood, where he restarted BlackTree. Tank and I continued our relationship off and on until I realized he could never give me the committed relationship I wanted. We kept in touch later in life, but I moved on.

One day while I was working at the retail store, I met an older White woman. She had a small stature with black hair. *Why was this old lady in the computer store?* I wondered. She was there getting a computer repaired. I asked her leading questions into why she was in the store with the goal of getting her interested in computer training. I showed her the catalog of courses and walked her around the training center. She was very engaged in the conversation.

"How long have you been at CompUSA?" she asked.

I had been there six months. She told me her office was right next door in one of the new office buildings built at the end of the shopping center. She went into her purse and pulled out a business card. I looked at it and read "Athena Computer Learning Center." That's when I realized she was trying to recruit me.

She said, "I would love to talk to you more about coming to work at Athena. We have an opening for a training consultant."

"I don't do the training," I told her.

She laughed and said, "That's just a funny name for a salesperson. They consult the clients on what training they need."

"Oh, okay," I said. "Is this for an interview?"

"Only if you want the job," she said. "You had me ready to buy training here, and I own a training business."

I called her and met three days later. I was hired at Athena and worked there for sixteen months.

I started at the end of 1999 when the world was freaking out about Y2K and a possible widespread computer programming shortcut that could cause havoc as the year changed at the turn of the millennium. Obviously, nothing happened, and I started the millennium in a new job. The building and the center were brand new. I was twenty-three and on a sales team with all White people (three men and two women) who were all in their forties with families. We sat in cubes in the far corner of the office past the training rooms. I kept conversations general and did not speak much about having graduated from Vanderbilt since they went to tech schools, the University of Tennessee, or no college. I downplayed Vanderbilt since I had experienced sideways comments about affirmative action in my earlier job. While working, I also continued to take technology courses like Office Suite, HTML, and website design. The work environment remained chill until I started to win big contracts.

"Let me show you the ropes, kid," said one of my male colleagues.

Sometimes I inherited companies that had been longtime clients just to be a point of contact. I was able to upsell these clients into a larger contract. One client company had the type of contract where employees could come for training once per year, which drew down the annual contract budget. I convinced the head of HR to invest in more Cisco Certified and Microsoft Certified Systems Engineers due to the high consulting fees they were paying to outsource those services. Through conversation, I pitched that developing this talent in-house would reduce their costs over time as well as make the company more secure without so many outside companies controlling their systems. These high-end training courses were the bread and butter at Athena. Securing an annual contract quadrupled the size of the budget, and I got a large commission check.

It also quadrupled the jealousy from the other salespeople. The companies they threw at me for customer service were now under more scrutiny. One sales guy who once worked on that client where I got the large contract tried to take credit for my work, saying, "I laid the groundwork." My position was he laid down on the job, and I scooped it up. I was no longer receiving sales tips. It was cool, though, because unbeknownst to them, I had other sales jobs. Again, I learned not to disclose too much when working with people, especially about my success. It just breeds envy, and I preferred to stay low-key and soak up whatever they wanted to teach me. I guess I had it honest. Aunt Daisy took a similar approach.

GET IT IN WRITING

In the spring of 2000, I applied to graduate school at the Peabody School of Education at Vanderbilt. I had learned so much about education and technology working in computer training sales at CompUSA and Athena that I wanted to learn more about how people learn with technology. I was over the moon to learn I was accepted and awarded a graduate assistantship that pays a small stipend to work for a professor and a tuition waiver so that my overall cost was decreased. I told my mother first. I would be the first person in my family to get an advanced degree. I planned at once to move out of my apartment and into a third bedroom at my mother's house in Nashville to reduce my expenses.

Two weeks later, I received an impersonal email from Peabody saying after a closer look at my undergraduate grades, they reversed my acceptance. I sat there staring at this email. I was livid. I called the school and asked who I could speak to about this matter. They told me to reply to the email, and they would send it on. I drafted an email telling them my grades were lower than I wanted them to be in undergrad because I had to work nearly thirty hours per week to take care of myself. I did not want to continue to take on more loans, and my mother did not have the resources to send me money. I essentially laid my grades at their feet. I worked hard in undergrad. I worked and ran an entertainment company. "Grades are not the only way to evaluate potential," I wrote in the letter. I sent it off and waited one day, then two days, and did not hear back.

I decided to go up to the administration office. They couldn't ignore me when I was sitting in their face. They said only the dean could decide to overturn my acceptance reversal.

"Excuse me, I really need to see the dean today," I said.

"Yes, he is in, but he is preparing for a long summer vacation," the secretary told me.

"Then I have to see him today. I will wait."

I waited for an hour and then the secretary took me into his office. I read him the letter and told him that had Vanderbilt provided more grants, I would not have had to work so much, and my grades would have been better. I pretty much demanded he overturn my denial and reinstate my assistantship.

"It was not fair to accept me and then deny me with a cold email," I firmly told him. "If I do not get at least a 3.5 grade point average, then you can pull the assistantship and waiver."

I will never forget the way he quietly sat there as I made my case. I could tell from his expression he could not believe this young Black woman was in his office, telling him what he was going to do.

I had no fear because I wanted to go to school, and I had already given up the apartment I loved to move in with my mother. I also mentioned I was first-generation, and Vanderbilt should be proud I wanted to return for another degree. Finally, I shut up and sat there, both of us staring at each other.

After what felt like forever, he responded with, "Okay."

He walked me out and told his admin to call the admissions office and tell them he felt I deserved to be in the fall class. Well, that was not going to work for me. I asked if I could get it in writing. I could tell by his facial expression it perturbed him. I said I would wait again. The admin wrote a letter, printed it, and he signed it as he ran out of the office to the airport.

I was reaccepted and did very well in graduate school. The lowest grade I received was an A- in an independent study course. My GPA was 3.966 when I graduated in December 2002. I learned one of the most important lessons in my life: to never, and I mean *never*, take a no from someone without the power to tell you yes. Had I accepted that benign denial via email, I probably would not have gone to graduate school. I also learned to get everything in writing. I gained so much confidence with my success through that challenge.

9/11

By the spring of 2001, the acceptance into graduate school was final, and I shared the news with my coworkers. About two weeks later, Athena laid me off. I do not know if that was their original plan, but knowing I was starting graduate school that fall meant I could not work full-time. I wasn't worried, though. Despite the economic downturn, I had been networking and planning, and by the time I started school in the fall, I had a job working for another technology company.

I moved in with my mother in July, which was a big change for me. I had been living on my own since 1994. It was nice to spend time with Momma and my brother, who also had his girlfriend, Tanya, and my three-year-old niece, Melony. I made those adjustments so I could focus on school without the burden of so many bills. For the Fourth of July, I flew to New Jersey to meet a guy I had befriended through a mentor. She was Nigerian and introduced me to her cousin, who was also Nigerian. We spoke on the phone for two months, and he offered to fly me to New Jersey to meet. He was a sweet person. He put me up in a hotel in Newark and showed me the town. We spent the days site-seeing, walking on the New Jersey pier, and eating at different restaurants. I have pictures with the World Trade Center behind me. We then took the subway to New York and walked through the lower-level stores under the World Trade Center. He bought me souvenirs, and we got ice cream before going into the World Trade Center for a tour.

We took the elevator up and then got into another elevator that took us to the top of the tower. There was a museum explaining the history of New York and playing music. I stepped into one of the seats next to the window, and it had a step down so you could see the city. My stomach dropped when I sat down. We were so high up. You could not make out people on the street below. I could see all of New York, and across the space I could see all of New Jersey. There were a hundred or so people in there with us. It was a great day. We left and had dinner. It was a successful and relaxing trip upon my arrival back in Nashville. I was in a period of exploration and dating for once. I was always in relationships, so it was nice just to date and have fun without it being serious. I had no idea at the time how memorable and tortuous the memory of that trip would be.

I remember September 11, 2001, so vividly.

8:50 a.m.: I am awakened by my brother telling me to turn on my TV in my room. Something happened in New York. I saw a replay of the first plane flying into the World Trade Center tower. The news was live, showing the smoke billowing from the building. They were reporting what they thought was a plane that malfunctioned.

9:03 a.m.: Another plane flew into the south tower. I screamed from the terror of watching this live. Then the news shifted, telling us this was not an accident and was a terrorist attack. Both towers were now on fire, and they had already deployed firefighters.

9:37 a.m.: A plane flies into the Pentagon. I was terrified now and called my mother at work. She said they were sending everyone home, and she was leaving at once. We were all huddled around the television, not sure what was happening.

I began to see little specks falling from the windows above the place where the fire was burning. I was sick when I realized people were jumping to their death. They could not get out. I recalled my experience at the tour of my stomach dropping from how high we were. I was traumatized imagining the decision those people made to burn or jump. Either way, they were going to die. Then what we could never have imagined happened.

9:59 a.m.: The south tower began to slowly fall, collapse, and pancake. Everyone in the house began to scream and cry. "Oh my god, oh my god, all those people."

10:03 a.m.: The plane crashes in Pennsylvania.

10:29 a.m.: The north tower collapses.

It was all too much. We thought the world was coming to an end.

It was palpable for me. I was just there. In that building. In the bottom and at the top two months before. I am a very empathetic person, and I kept reliving my experience and seeing what those people saw jumping to their death. Having my graduate education start with 9/11 changed my outlook on life. I realized life is fleeting. I mean, I was just there, and now I was watching terrorists destroy an almost impenetrable set of buildings in a terrorist attack.

Nearly twenty years later, there is still speculation on who did it, why, and how, but it changed America, and it changed me. I finished graduate school in December of 2002 with a Master's in Education and Technology. I was the first and maybe the only person to ever get that degree from Vanderbilt. I was twenty-five and in love. I moved to Minneapolis, Minnesota, to live with my high school sweetheart, Oliver. I had a job and was starting a whole new life. The future was promising, but you don't know sweet without also tasting what bitter is.

CHAPTER 7

Minneapolis

The next phase of my life in Minneapolis would last seven years, challenge my family dynamics, and bring me to my knees.

I was visiting Chicago with my mother the summer prior to starting graduate school in 2001. I was curious about Oliver, who I dated up until the summer before college. I was curious about how he was doing. My mother and I were coming from the south Chicago suburbs visiting family. This area was very close to where Oliver and his family lived. I thought his stepfather might still live there.

I said, sort of talking to myself, "We should drive that way."

My mother, in her clairvoyant voice, said, "We should. He is probably outside."

About a block from the house, I could see Oliver's stepfather outside working on the lawn. I honked my horn, yelling, "Hello, Mr. Hargett!"

He turned and gave a big smile. He waved us over, so we parked and came over to the house. He gave me a big hug.

"Tiff and Shirley, it is so good to see y'all. I have not seen you, Tiff, since you and O graduated from high school. How are things? Where are you living?"

Oliver's family and friends called him "O," so I'll refer to him throughout as O.

My mom and I shared with Mr. Hargett that we lived in Nashville and I was starting graduate school in a few weeks. He shared in the pride my mother felt. Mr. Hargett said, "I am sure O would love to hear from you."

"Really? How is he? Where is he?" I asked. "I heard on the news about what happened at FAMU (Florida A&M University)." Oliver was facing accusations of participating in a gang rape of a girl in the apartment he shared with some roommates.

Mr. Hargett gave me a solemn look, saying, "Yeah, that whole thing really set him back. He had to leave school and is living in Minneapolis with Lea (his mother). He could really use a good friend. He lost his education with those allegations. Even though we know he did not rape the girl, it still ruined his reputation and education. He tried to stay there, but then he got depressed, so Lea had him leave school."

"Wow," was all I could say. I did not want to comment on the incident, which triggered my own hidden hurt, so I just said, "Minneapolis! Why there?"

Mr. Hargett said, "You know, the divorce was rough, and Lea wanted to start over somewhere."

I then asked about Jae and Grant, Oliver's siblings. "Jae and Grant are doing well. They were here for a few weeks this summer," he said. "Jae is eleven and Grant is thirteen."

"Man!" I responded. "I love those kids. Well, here is my cell phone number. You can tell O I said hello."

I did not want to seem too interested even though I rode by hoping to reconnect with Oliver. We gave another hug, and Momma and I kept on moving across town and made it to Hyde Park further north. It was only an hour later when I received a call with a 952 (Minnesota) area code. My stomach dropped when I picked up and heard Oliver's deep raspy voice.

"What's up, Tiff?" asked Oliver.

Trying to sound chill, I said, "Living life. How are you?"

"I'm good," he said.

So I asked, "How is living in Minneapolis?"

"It's okay. I'm working for Ma," was all he said.

"Cool. Well, I am out with my mother, so I should call you another time," not sure what else to say.

"Please tell her hello," was his response.

I said, "Will do. Talk to you soon."

He said, "Looking forward to it."

"Okay, bye." I had to end the call because I was overly nervous, and it was awkward. I did think about him saying "looking forward to it," but I did not call him until I returned to Nashville. We regularly talked from then on. We reminisced about high school. I even read him the letter he wrote to me when we attended the Christ and Others retreat where we first began "liking" each other. I visited him in Minneapolis that Thanksgiving to see what he was up to. It was so good to see him and the family. They were living in a beautiful mission-style home in the upscale Golden Valley suburb of Minneapolis. Lea, his mother, had also reconnected with an old boyfriend, Ralph, whom she knew from her younger days in Chicago. The entire family was living there with him in Minneapolis. Mr. Hargett left that part out. Even though I was still dating other people, seeing Oliver and the family had me catching feelings for him again.

His mother was very endearing to me during that trip. I always looked up to her and sought her approval when I dated O in high school. I idealized her as a goal for this upper-class dream I had for myself. She owned a manufacturing company now, and Oliver was working for her in information technology. During the week there, I began to visualize myself being part of this beautiful family and perhaps moving to Minneapolis.

I also traveled to Minneapolis for spring break in 2002. His mother connected me with a city council office, and I took an internship that summer in the Minneapolis City Council office of Robert Lilligren. He was the earliest First Nation elected official in Minneapolis. I worked on projects and aided his senior policy aide, Andrea Jenkins, who was friends with Lea. Andrea would go on to become the first openly transgender elected official in the nation in 2018.

INTERNING IN CITY COUNCIL

That summer with the city council was a huge learning experience. I started with shadowing Andrea for the first couple of weeks. I went to this neighborhood and that neighborhood. I heard about all the issues with potholes, streetlights, predatory tow companies, drugs, gangs, immigrant concerns from them and about them, and the need for more local jobs. I asked a ton of questions about how the office deals with these issues. Overall, shadowing Andrea was exhausting, so I asked Connie, our office manager, what else she needed help with. I stuck closer to the office and began answering the phones and sitting in on Robert's meetings.

One of those meetings was with V.J. Smith, a community organizer involved in MAD DADS. MAD DADS is an acronym for Men Against Destruction-Defending Against Drugs and Social-Disorder. MAD DADS, INC. was founded in May of 1989 by a group of concerned Omaha, Nebraska, parents fed up with gang violence and the flow of illegal drugs in their community. V.J. would go on to lead the Minneapolis chapter and became the national president for years. At that meeting, he was pitching an idea for a community festival. Robert suggested I work with V.J. on the festival. He and I worked for six weeks, and we pulled off the first Annual Southside Community Festival. I went on to program up to the fourth annual festival before moving on from the city council.

V.J. and I are still great friends. He is one of the most caring and committed people I know. He was there for me later in my time in Minneapolis when I went through a personal crisis.

Nearing graduation from Vanderbilt, Oliver wanted me to move to Minneapolis. The only way that would be possible was for him to get an apartment and move out of the house he was living in with his mother. I wish I had seen the writing on the wall that his moving did not occur until I was there that summer. I did the most, as they say, in this relationship. But I was in love and did not see the obvious. We moved into an apartment in St. Louis Park, a suburb of Minneapolis. I should have seen he was not motivated and independent enough without me there. I should have seen I was pushing him and would need to keep pushing him for the rest of our relationship. It never occurred to me to move into my own apartment and see if he could take care of himself.

I moved to Minneapolis in December of 2002. One of the advantages of living in Minneapolis was occasionally seeing my dad. He did the Chicago to Seattle route for years as a porter for Amtrak. On my second day in Minneapolis, he was coming through St. Paul, where the Amtrak station was. I made my way around 7:00 a.m. to meet him. The roads were icy. Five cars had spun out along the highway. I was already nervous because I had not seen my dad in years, and now

I had to contend with scary icy roads. I started to slide on the ice, and a car hit me from behind, but the damage was minor. I pulled over, and we exchanged information. But I was determined to see my dad, so I kept going. I saw my dad that day, but only for ten minutes by the time I made it there. It was an awkward meeting because we had not seen each other since 1995 when I was in Chicago for the summer after my first year of college. We had sporadic phone calls after 1995. Prior to moving to Minneapolis, I told him he would need to be more consistent in my life and I still needed a father, even though I was an adult.

In the coming years, I would see my dad about once a month on his way from Chicago to Seattle or on the trip home. And sometimes, he would sneak me on the train in the private sleeper cars, and I would travel back with him to Chicago. In May of 2003, I walked for my graduate degree from Peabody School of Education at Vanderbilt University. My dad came from Chicago, and he drove my cousin Devoy. It was the first time in my life he was able to celebrate one of my accomplishments. It was so special to Momma, my dad, Oliver, my brother Bernard, and my niece Melony as well as other family to see me graduate.

Dad would always bring me little gifts from his travels. He once brought me a huge box of king crabs and shrimp from Seattle for my birthday in 2004. I made an incredible gumbo for my birthday/SuperBowl dinner party. We rebuilt our relationship over those years, and I am so grateful for those short visits. I feel my move to Minneapolis was a gift from God to give me the opportunity to reconnect with my father.

WORKING IN MINNEAPOLIS

Through connections made in the city council, I got a job working for the Midtown Greenway Coalition as a transit program manager. I worked with great people, including Theresa Nelson and Tim Springer, who was the executive director. The Greenway was an old train corridor that was now a biking path with the plans for a future streetcar to be there. My job was to create a campaign to market this developing streetcar line and successfully get resolutions passed in sixteen neighborhoods along with Midtown Greenway to support the streetcar line. I also planned an annual meeting for the coalition in the soon to be renovated Sears building that would become the Midtown Exchange.

I worked there for eleven months before being appointed to policy aide for the same council member, Robert Lilligren, whom I interned with after Andrea took another position outside of the council. I was hesitant to take the appointment because of the way Andrea did the job—she was everywhere and knew everyone. Andrea assured me I could make the position my own and do it my way. I did exactly that. Soon after starting, our office became the first office to use a smartphone under my suggestion. Robert was able to respond to emails on the go, which in 2004 was revolutionary. We were able to be super-efficient and responsive. I sat on task forces, including the development of the 3-1-1 system and the youth development board. My proudest achievement was taking part in the development of the Midtown Exchange, which was a one-million-plus square foot former Sears building which sat dark and blighted for eleven years. One of Robert's campaign goals was its redevelopment.

During the process of meeting with the contractor and developer, minority contractors complained they were left out of participating because the bonding and insurance was too expensive. I posed a question to the developer, wondering if those contracts could be issued in smaller amounts to allow more small subcontractors to benefit from the project. Ryan Companies, the developer, was able to do this, resulting in many minority contractors' participation. The project also greatly surpassed its minority hiring goals. Robert won an award from Minority Supplier Development Council because seventeen million in revenue was won by minority contractors in the project due to the contracts being broken into smaller pieces.

It took some time for me to meet friends in Minneapolis, but in 2003, I received an invitation to an event about school choice that would impact my life and career direction. School choice is a term for public education options, describing a wide array of programs offering students and their families voluntary alternatives to publicly provided schools, to which students are generally assigned by the location of their family residence. In some areas based on their school choice laws, parents could choose the school for their child without a dependency on geography, but they or the school would be responsible for transportation.

School choice allows public education funds to follow students to the schools or services that best fit their needs—whether that's to a public school, private school, charter school, home school, or any other learning environment families choose. At that event, I heard Dr. Howard Fuller speak for the first time. Dr. Fuller was the founder of the

Black Alliance for Educational Options (BAEO), a national nonprofit focused on helping Black parents create more options for Black students.

At that event, I met Chanda Smith. She was a single mom and working at a nonprofit in North Minneapolis. She and I would become good friends and go on to meet with Dr. Fuller often and cofound the Minneapolis Chapter of the Black Alliance for Educational Options with Sondra Hollinger-Samuels, another leading Black woman in Minneapolis. We traveled to our first BAEO conference in 2005 in Detroit.

We advocated for school choice legislation in Minnesota and made waves as we sat at the table with Republicans to ensure school choice policies were equitable. Sometimes they called us the "right-wing ladies" because, at that time, school choice was considered conservative until the Obama era when those policies shifted a bit leftward. Dr. Fuller taught us that "there are no permanent friends, just permanent interests," so we made sure to be at the table where our interests and those affecting our community were making decisions. It did not matter what people tried to call us; our interests were Black children having the best options available to them. Chanda married Roland Baker in 2008 and has continued to grow in her career in Minneapolis.

MOTHERHOOD

In the Fall of 2003, Oliver and I were in love and living our life happily together. He worked for his mother at her company, and I was transitioning from the Midtown Greenway

Coalition to Minneapolis City Council. I was twenty-eight, and we found out we were expecting a son. Oliver proposed to me on Thanksgiving when my momma and my niece, Melony, were visiting. It was a surprise, but I know his mother pressured him to propose. I was still happy about it, and it made me feel better about being pregnant. My pregnancy was easy. I was healthy with no morning sickness. I tried to cover up my pregnancy to become more indispensable at the city council, but by my fourth month, there was no more hiding. We were deep into the Minneapolis winter, and my big sweaters could not sufficiently conceal my growing belly. When Robert and Connie took me out for my birthday lunch in January, I told them I was expecting in July. They were very happy for me. I continued working at the city council the whole time up until my parental leave.

One of my favorite times while pregnant was my trip to Chicago and Nashville. I took the Amtrak to Chicago and had a private sleeping car. I was six months pregnant, and it was just my unborn baby and me. He and I were in tune. He was so active, always jumping around in my tummy. It was such a special time to spend traveling and reflecting and writing in my journal on the train ride. My family had not seen me pregnant or much since I had been in Minneapolis. I stayed with my cousin, Sharron "Dottie" Downs, for three days in Chicago. I enjoyed the time sitting at her kitchen table and talking all morning. I flew to Nashville, where my mother and brother lived, and my aunts were coming up from Atlanta to celebrate my arrival. We had a big family dinner. I then flew back to Chicago. Being six months pregnant caught up with me. I was exhausted, so I got back on the train a day early and returned to Minneapolis.

Oliver and I came back to Chicago later in May for a baby shower given by the Chicago family and hosted at Dottie's house. My dad was there and my half-sister Nia and all my best friends, Vikki, Nikki, and Anisha. Oliver and I had a load of presents to take back to Minneapolis. We could barely fit everything in the car. I also had a baby shower at work in city council before I went on parental leave at the end of June 2004.

I was going to see my midwife weekly. On my thirty-eighth week, I mentioned to the midwife that the baby was not moving as much. She told me to count the kicks and not to worry because he had less room to wiggle. I felt okay about that. The coming week was my last week at work, and I was busy completing projects and training my replacement. I was not as present with the baby's movements, and I was moving around so much. I was due on July 9, 2004. Right after the Fourth of July, I was scheduled to go in for my thirty-nine-week appointment.

I was nervous about this appointment because I had not felt the baby move in a few days. Oliver and his younger sister, Jae, came with me to the appointment. The doctor did the standard measurements and went to check the heartbeat with the doppler. She went around and around my stomach, but all you could hear was the *shuuh* sound of the doppler, but no heartbeat.

"Oh," she said, "this one must be low on batteries." She left the room and came back with another one. Still no heartbeat. I was tensing up but trying to be brave for Jae because she had never been to an appointment before. The midwife told me she would feel better if we went to the obstetrics department for a full ultrasound.

We walked across the hospital without saying a word. I was terrified but figured everything would be okay. Maybe the baby was just backward, or the machines were not working properly. All three of us walked into the ultrasound room. A doctor I had never met did the full ultrasound, moving the wand slowing and methodically across my huge belly. After covering my stomach twice, she wiped me off and put the wand up. I do not remember breathing through the whole inspection. She looked at Oliver and then at me. My brain could not understand what she said. He turned to me and grabbed my hand tight.

She said some euphemism like "sweetie" or something, and then: "I can't find the baby's heartbeat. He is gone."

I finally took a breath before letting out a single cry.

"I don't understand," Oliver said. "What do you mean?"

She said, "Sometimes these things happen, and we do not know why." Earlier in the pregnancy, we were given the opportunity to do genetic testing, and we decided against it. "There could have been a complication," said the doctor.

I felt so puzzled and lost. She told Oliver I needed to be checked in so they could induce me. She did not know how long the baby had been deceased, and there was a risk of me getting an infection as he decayed.

"How long do we have?" Oliver asked.

"Please be back by tomorrow," she said.

I don't remember much after that. Next thing, I was in our apartment, in my bed, sobbing. Oliver called Lea and Ralph and told them the news. They came over right away. He then called my mother, and she made plans to fly to Minneapolis from Nashville early the next morning.

We checked into the hospital the next day. They put me in a special wing away from the other mothers having babies, so I did not have to hear the crying. It was all so surreal. I was supposed to be having my baby. Now, I was having my baby, but he won't get to come home with me. I was induced with Pitocin and Cytotec. Early the next morning, I pushed him out, and they handed me a beautiful baby boy. He was so warm and moist. Oliver cut the umbilical cord, and I cradled him in my arms. He had jet black wavy hair like Oliver's. His face was my shape, and he had my fat cheeks and small ears. He was beautiful. But now, he was an angel. One of the other special services they offered was a photographer. She came in after they cleaned me and the baby up. I was able to put a onesie on him and a little bonnet and wrapped him in a blanket.

Oliver and I took pictures with Oliver Louis Hargett IV, and then my momma and Lea held him while the photographer took pictures. Everyone left Oliver and me alone. We just stared at baby Oliver and cradled him so gently. We had so many dreams of this little guy growing up and running around. We had so many dreams for our life together. I was befuddled. I could not cry. I did my duty. I brought him into the world. He experienced a train ride, a plane ride. He ate good, and he was loved and expected by so many. I kept feeling his face and his hand. He was turning cold.

The nurse entered the room and told us we had about thirty minutes before they needed to take him to the morgue. Lea and my mother had already arranged for the funeral home to pick up the baby. He would be cremated. I opted not to do an autopsy, so we never had a definitive prognosis of what happened. Oliver's siblings were in the waiting area, so we let them back to see the baby. They cried softly, trying hard not to upset us.

Everyone else returned to the room. The nurse looked at Oliver. He held me tight and said, "It's time." I then began to cry. I did not want to let him go.

"My baby," I cried out.

I came home, and the pain was unbearable. I was going through all the physical changes of a new mother, but there was no baby. There was a darkness surrounding me, and I just could not shake it. My breasts were sore and engorged. I had to get in the shower and press out the milk to get any relief. It was so sad to watch my milk wash down the drain. There is no preparation for the grief I felt. I just cried myself to sleep repeatedly. My momma stayed with us for about a week after we got home.

I did discover in my postnatal care I had an issue where my blood did not have enough of a certain protein. My blood was thick and clotted the placenta, which led to the baby not getting enough oxygen.

For a few days, I was able to focus my attention on the memorial. Lea and Ralph opened their home and backyard for the ceremony. I was numb and sad, but it was hard for me to sit back and do nothing as everyone tried so hard to make me feel better. They worked so hard to prepare the yard for everyone. We had a beautiful well attended memorial for the baby. The mayor of Minneapolis attended and over fifty friends. It was truly beautiful. I have a DVD of it but have not had the courage to rewatch it. The planning helped divert my grief enough to get through a few days, but afterward, I went back into the darkness.

I started to see a therapist soon after to help me with my depression, which I could not shake. I was in a bad place. I was suicidal during that time after losing the baby. I saw the therapist for, ultimately, the next four years. Dr. Taborn was an older African American male psychologist and, at the time, the only one in Minneapolis. He became like a grandfather to me. He helped me direct my depression, work through other issues, and get a plan about my relationship with Oliver, which descended into an abyss after losing baby Oliver. Dr. Taborn also helped me move my career in the direction I was enthusiastic about.

I was angry with God at that time. Why did he take my baby? Feeling that way was difficult for me, because God and I had always had a tight connection. As a way out of this rut, I started reading the lost books of the bible, like Barnabas. I visited churches and regularly attended a nondenominational church that was urban and cool with a good message. At two years out from losing the baby, I was still trying to shake the blues. Oliver stopped progressing after we lost the baby. Physically he was always complaining of back pains, and emotionally he and I were on two different levels. He was a hermit and had stopped working. He stayed home while I was working and traveling all the time with my new career with Fielding Nair International (FNI).

Fielding Nair International was an educational architecture firm. I met the president, Randy Fielding, through my research on interior design and educational spaces. I reached out and met with him. His firm designed a large project in my city council ward. I did a consulting project for FNI where I coordinated a training for a group of Australian educators to come to Minneapolis in January of 2007. It was a great success, and Randy asked me to join the firm as an educational planning consultant. From April 2007 to November 2008, I would fly over 89,000 miles while consulting on projects across the USA and in the Cayman Islands. I traveled Monday to Thursday and came home over the weekends. Dr. Taborn helped me figure out this career move, and it was an exciting transition, but I was still supporting us alone. Oliver had severe back pains and got a medical diagnosis, but the damage and stress from losing a child and carrying us financially were too much on me.

The only thing Oliver and I had in common during this period was our research on what some might call "conspiracy theories" and trying to discover how the world really works. This research initially made me question God and my significance as a human being. But as I researched further and read more and watched videos, and bought the books they referenced, I learned God was more central to the working of the world than I had ever imagined. I learned those in power were hiding great religious secrets, and I mean everything was connected. My relationship with God was in a place of discovery. Trying to find the truth. Trying to understand where I needed to be and go.

Oliver eventually told me he was not ready to get married. That was not a shock. One day, while I was at home and Oliver was out, he left his laptop open, and I heard it ping. His Gmail popped up. I only glanced over but was taken aback when I noticed a conversation with a woman named Kera, which had seventeen messages. Then I looked and saw other extensive conversations between them. I clicked on the first message.

It said, "I feel bad about what you and I did in Tiffany's house." He was cheating, but it was over anyway. The clock was running out on my time in Minneapolis.

In January of 2008, I was traveling on business to my hometown of Chicago. My best friend, Anisha, came to stay with me in my hotel room. We were chatting it up like only BFFs can do. During this conversation, I was expressing my frustration about Oliver.

As I stood in the window overlooking the frozen Lake Michigan, I screamed, *"God, where is my husband?"* At that moment, I decided to leave that relationship for good and to move back to Chicago. I had planned to move in July.

I came back to Chicago in April and saw over twenty condos before finally putting one under lease in Hyde Park. It met all my needs. It was a secure building with video monitoring from the television to see who was at the door. It had a workout room as well as a parking space I could see from the balcony. Of course, it had a large closet, a nice bathroom, and a small room I could use as an office. The kitchen was open with newer stainless appliances. The condo had been vacant for over a year. The owner was excited to have a tenant. There was a nice coffee shop just a block away. It was my dream place to start my life over in Chicago. I paid a $1,400 down payment and returned to Minneapolis to plan my move in July.

In May, I traveled to Nashville for my Auntie Debbie's son Kevin Jr.'s graduation from high school. My aunts, Melody, Delovely, and Robbin, came up from Atlanta. I was excited about the move back to Chicago, but my momma, brother, his daughters, and three of my aunts were in the South. I would still be eight hours from my momma. I did not know what to do about that.

I went back to Minneapolis, and one night as I was sleeping, I had a dream God told me to go to Atlanta. He told me my husband would be there. I woke up and said, "Okay, God, I will be obedient."

It was so direct and powerful I knew not to question it. I was obedient and called my realtor in Chicago. I told her I could not take the loft. She asked why.

"My job is changing, and I cannot move to Chicago," I told her. She called the owner and offered me even more time because the place had been vacant for so long. I said I could not take it. He returned my full deposit. I guess God was making this easy. I then called my Aunt Melody in Atlanta and asked her if I could stay in her extra room. She said, "Of course." I packed up what I could fit in my Acura and put the rest in storage, and on June 26, 2008, I set out and drove from Minneapolis to Louisville to Chicago and then to Atlanta. I was single but not quite free. Hallelujah!

PHOTOS (CHAPTER 1–7)

THESE PHOTOS ARE TO ENHANCE
THE STORY AND BE A HISTORICAL
RECORD OF THESE TIMES.

Little Shirley, Wilbur Green Sr., Wilbur "Sweetie" Green Jr. and Shirley Green, 1954.

Uncle Sweetie, age three and little Shirley, age two, 1955.

Little Shirley at twenty-five, 1978.

Uncle Sweetie was killed in 1992 in Chicago.

All the sisters: Robbin, Melody, Delovely, Valerie, Deborah, and Shirley in 2017 after the funeral for Valerie's son, Devoy. My cousin and soul brother, Devoy, died from complications twenty years after being shot in a drive-by. He was paraplegic. He was a cherished member of our family and community.

Baby Tiffany 1976   My dad's twin, Earnest.

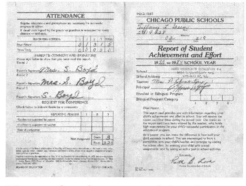

Young Vernest   My second grade report card signed
Cantrell.   by Grandma.

Shirley and Jesse were   All of Shirley and Jesse's Children
a beautiful couple and   and Jesse's Children (Shirley
made beautiful children.   is missing).

Mar, "92"

Grandma a few months
before she passed.

Muhammad Speaks ad. First
full-page advertisement for
the bean pie, June 1970.

Grandma was always the life of the party. Here with her
grandson Bernard; granddaughter Camilla.

Auntie Valerie and little Tiffany.

Momma (Shirley Green Wallace) being celebrated at CNA Insurance where she worked for twenty-plus years.

Little Tiff.

Age ten.

Tiffany's birthday, four or five, and cousin Camilla.

Momma, Tiffany age six, Bernard age one.

Tiffany sixteen, Bernard eleven.

Tiffany was six, Devoy was five, Camilla was three, and Bernard one.

Halloween at the family building off Stony Island in Chicago, 1982. These were just the children from our block. We used to have so much fun.

My seventh birthday. Devoy was always by my side.

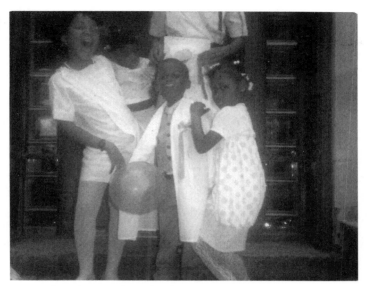

Bernard graduating from kindergarten.

Momma, Bernard, and me after his graduation
from kindergarten.

Momma, Bernard, and me, Easter, 1985.

Momma, Bernard, and I took family pictures when I visited
Nashville from Minneapolis in 2004 when I was pregnant.

Bernard's fourth birthday.

Christmas, 1986.

Sixth grade class picture at St. Cyril.

Tiffany with classmates. I was always taking pictures.

Ms. Peaches with classmates.

St. Cyril School, Ms. Peaches in the peach sweater and Ms. Duncan in the red sweater.

Classmates from St. Cyril, eighth grade, 1990.

My eighth-grade class photo, 1990.

St. Cyril class of 1990.

Giving the valedictorian speech.

Giving my momma a flower during graduation. Auntie DeDe brought me flowers. Ms. Peaches is in the background. We had an incredible school and church community.

Proud day for Momma.

Momma's best friend Barbara and her son, Tanzel, came.

The whole family was there; Debbie, Robbin, DeDe, and Devoy.

Family classic moment: The entire family went on vacation to
Wisconsin Dells. This is all the kids performing Bobby Brown's
"My prerogative," 1988.

Performing "Good Hair, Bad Hair" from *School Daze*, 1989. I'm in the red on the left.

Dancer in *The Wiz* at St. Ignatius, playing the wind, 1993.

We performed "I Don't Want to be Alone Tonight" from School Daze. Erica, Tiffany, and Sherise. Sherise's mother made the dresses. We did not play around for talent shows at St. Cyril.

Performing "You Remind Me" by Mary J. Blige in 1992 at a St. Cyril Talent show with Vikki and Fesha.

I performed in *Hair*, *The Wiz*, and *Fiddler on the Roof* at St. Ignatius. Those plays earned me induction into the Thespian Society. I continued performing into adulthood.

The International Thespian Society
A component of the Educational Theatre Association
3368 CENTRAL PARKWAY, CINCINNATI, OHIO 45225-2392
THIS CERTIFIES THAT

TIFFANY GREEN
FOR MERITORIOUS PARTICIPATION IN THEATRICAL ARTS,
IS A MEMBER OF INTERNATIONAL THESPIAN SOCIETY
TROUPE NUMBER 3515

L i f e t i m e   M e m b e r

Performer in professional African Dance Troupe in Nashville while in College at Vanderbilt.

Cheerleader for St. Ignatius.

The family after graduation from St. Ignatius. (Nikki, Melody, Debbie, Vikki, Bernard, James, DeDe, Devoy, Momma, and Daisy).

Getting ready to leave for graduation from St. Ignatius College Prep in Chicago.

Black Student Weekend '94
Vanderbilt University
Tiffany
Tiffany Green
Chicago, Illinois

Name tag from Black Student Weekend at Vanderbilt University, 1994.

Vikki and Tiffany, 1993.

Vikki's wedding, 1995.

Momma and me before I went
to prom, 1994.

Auntie Valerie, Devoy, Ladena,
and me, pre-prom.

Uncle James and Auntie Robbin and me.   Prom photo.
James drove me to Vanderbilt.

The entire family and friends (Vikki and her mom) came out to see me off for prom. I wonder if Jesse still has that video.

Anisha, Devoy, and   Anisha's eighth grade graduation, with
me, May 17, 1996.   her brothers, Anwar and Chuckie, 1987.

Anisha and me, 2002.

Anisha's wedding.

Anisha and her daughter, Fallon.

Working as a flooring consultant at a high-end flooring store in Brentwood, Tennessee, 1995.

College was the change of scenery I needed to forget about what I left in Chicago.

Seeing Devoy for the first time after he
became paralyzed when I came home
for Christmas break, 1994.

Tiffany,
age nineteen.

College was
the break I
needed to have
fun and just
be myself. My
Vandy big sisters
from Georgia,
Latrice, Kim,
and Rochelle.

Delta party at Vanderbilt,
1994. We were having a ball.

Latrice and Kim invited me to
Atlanta for Freaknic in 1995.

I became a Sigma Silhouette, an auxiliary group of Phi Beta Sigma fraternity.

The Black Graduate Ceremony at Vanderbilt was more special than the regular graduation for me.

Jamaal Finkley and me on our way to a Vandy homecoming ball, 1994.

The whole family came to Nashville for the first college graduation for the family. I was so excited to see granddaddy Jesse Boyd attend.

Auntie Melody
and granddaddy.

I toured the World Trade
Center towers in New York
in July 2001. This was taken
on the New Jersey side before
taking the subway to the
building. I had PTSD after the
attacks because I remember my
stomach dropping when I sat
in the observation window at
the top.

Bernard and me, 1997.

Bernard and his
daughter, Melony,
1999.

Melony and her twin sisters, Kaylyn and Jaylyn.

My niece Melony and me, 1999.

Melony and me when her and Momma visited me in Minneapolis, 2002. I love being an aunt because of how important my aunts have been in my life.

The twins, Kaylyn and Jaylyn, and Robbin. Bernard has four girls.

Mom, Melony, and I went to Disney World in 2005 to celebrate Mom's retirement.

Bernard, Mom, and me, 2018.

Momma and her granddaughters, Kaylyn, Jaylyn, Melony, and Robbin, 2019.

I took photos of my oldest niece, Melony, in 2021 so she could update her social media. She graduates from college in May 2022. I am so proud and excited.

Mom and me when I visited Nashville in July 2020 to interview her in person for the book. I hadn't seen her since January 2020.

First picture with both parents as an adult at Graduate school graduation from Peabody at Vanderbilt.

I was the first to graduate from college and graduate school in the Green/ Boyd family.

Graduate school ceremony. Dad, Bernard, and Devoy in the background.

The family in Nashville when I visited while pregnant in 2004 (Valerie with twin granddaughters, Na'Dreyah and Na-Ryah, Auntie Melody, Auntie DeDe, Auntie Debbie, Melony, Jasmine, Auntie Robbin, Delovely, Camilla, and Momma).

The Aunties and me in
Nashville, 2004.

My dad and sister, Nia,
attended.

Playing games at the Chicago baby shower for me hosted at
Cousin Dottie's house, 2004.

Walking in a parade for the Midtown Greenway Coalition as Transportation Program Manager, i.e., dressed as a streetcar.

Article about the Midtown Greenway and cultural equity.

Jennifer White and me hosting the Black Alliance for
Educational Options booth at the Minneapolis fourth Annual
Southside Community Festival in 2005.

Article I wrote for the Midtown Greenway's newsletter, 2003.

Article on streetcar research.

Article about Chanda Smith and me and the work we were doing with BAEO (Black Alliance for Educational Options).

Article about school choice in Minneapolis.

I visited Minneapolis for Chanda's wedding, 2008.

Working in Cayman Islands for Fielding Nair International, 2005.

PART 4

RETURNING TO THE SOUTH AND RECOVERING OUR HERITAGE

CHAPTER 8

Atlanta

—

The day I left Minneapolis was like an exhale after holding my breath for seven years. I grew professionally, but I lost so much personally and needed to re-access that aspect of my life. I had gone through a transformation coming out of counseling because of my grief and depression the prior four years. I finally felt strong again by June 2008 when I set out on my own. This girl just wanted to have fun. I was so excited when I hit the highway under that auspiciously warm blue sky. I put one mile after the next as I traveled from Minneapolis to Chicago, then Nashville, and finally to Atlanta in my old Acura, packed to the brim with my essentials in hack-sacks or green army duffels. I was almost reversing the migration Aunt Daisy took in 1933 from Detroit to Chicago. I intended to start over and move to a more culturally diverse city with a growing economy. At first that was Chicago, but with Momma and Bernard in Nashville, I was still too far. I did not want to go live in Nashville again. With three aunts in Atlanta, I set out for the "Black mecca."

My first goal was to further my career in education, technology, and design. The work I did in Minneapolis was unique and would set the tone for my future in Atlanta. I took time to relax in between trips with Fielding Nair International, which were reducing in frequency. By fall, the economy dipped into a recession, and the firm lost many of its contracts. They let me go, but with a nice severance check. This allowed me to take some much-needed time off to explore Atlanta from November 2008 through January 2009.

I was thirty-two when I arrived in Atlanta, and all the relationships up to the point had not panned out. The years in Minneapolis with O needed too much of my time, financial resources, and energy. I left Minneapolis feeling depreciated. My primary desire was stability from a relationship. This steered me, as I discovered through therapy with Dr. Taborn. At that time, I was reconnecting off and on with my father, and this modulated my heart back into needing and receiving love.

Unfortunately, I was still on the hook for rent in Minneapolis since I was on the lease, and breaking that lease would have messed up my credit. Oliver was not meeting his obligation of sharing the expenses, but I was making enough money to pay the Minneapolis rent *and* give my aunt rent for the room. I was also paying the car note on the Honda Civic also in my name.

I did what I thought I needed to do, but I made a promise to myself in my next relationship, we would live off what the man made. I was not going to support a man again without him putting in equal effort. It does nothing for him except make him lazy, and it made me lose respect for Oliver. I knew he was dealing with health issues, and it was being managed. He was also seeing Dr. Taborn, but he just would not push himself, which is why Dr. Taborn coached me to leave.

If I could lose a baby and pick myself up, change my career and travel all over the world to make a living, he could find a job somewhere. He could have done something to help me, or rather, help us. I don't know if he was jealous or resentful toward me about the success I was having despite everything, but just like all the women before me, we get it done. We might go through trauma, but we don't die. We don't stop progressing even through the pain. I could not focus on his issues so much that I lost myself.

Even while I was in Atlanta and paying the rent and car note for him, he could have shown movement, any gesture of self-respect. Nothing. I came back to Minneapolis for Chanda's wedding in September 2008. The lease was ending, so I wanted to make sure the apartment was in order to get my deposit back. I came over with Chanda and Jennifer to pack. He was so belligerent to us there was no respect left to give. I walked away and never looked back.

DATING IN ATL

The first person I dated in Atlanta was a guy who was deceptively sweet, smart, and entrepreneurial—and sneaky. For that reason, I will not be using his name but will refer to him as HE. I wish him the best, but that relationship was just a rest stop. "All things sweet come with a little salty." We were a powder keg, so we had no future together. I learned some important lessons in a short period. One being I needed to be more specific when seeking a mate. HE was very controlling, and after six months, it was over.

Since I was seven years old, I have kept a journal. Each one could be a book, but the next time period of my life I documented so well I decided to share them in this book.

Here are my journal entries from a historic time in my life. I turned the page on love and started building the life I had dreamed of—and God promised me.

JANUARY 20, 2009, TUESDAY, 11:11 P.M.
Barack Obama's inauguration was today. I was in awe of him and his family. Especially his wife. She grew up on the southside of Chicago, just like me, and now she is the first lady. It blew my mind seeing him take the oath of office. A Black man is the president of the United States. I could not have even imagined this four years ago.

JANUARY 29, 2009, THURSDAY, 8:32 P.M.
Today is my thirty-third birthday. I don't feel thirty-three. I would say twenty-five. I'm feeling better emotionally since last week. I feel this is my year of new beginnings. I am in transition and have only been in Atlanta for six months or so. I am dating someone, but he is only talk, and I know it is not destined to last. All the promises have not amounted to much. I fell for his charm because I was too desperate for rest and relaxation. But nothing is easy or free. I must maintain my independence because I don't want to be under his control. He makes me feel nervous and on edge at least once a day.

Granted, I can mouth off, and I like to say what I want, but I don't deserve to be controlled. Life is too short. As soon as I get on my feet again, I will decide what to do. He does try to do nice things for me, but he talks under his breath, and we argue all the time. We are right back where we started this year. February 21 would make six months. I know this is not a healthy relationship, and it's time to get out.

FEBRUARY 2, 2009, MONDAY, 5:20 P.M.
Today I applied for jobs. I made a vow I would not get angry today no matter what he said to me. It seems like we have hit a crossroads in our relationship. I think I have pushed him to the edge. He's starting to get fed up with me (ditto). I know I tend to push to see how far I can go. He told me he was getting fed up. Maybe I want him to do what I don't feel strong enough to do… say this is not working out. It's nearly six months, and I don't have a clear answer. I want things to be easier, but he has lost most of his properties, and the financial pressure is taking a toll on him. We don't really do anything, so I am a bit underwhelmed by this whole thing. He is a good man, though.

"Love is lak de sea. It's uh movin' thing, but still and all, it takes its shape from de shore it meets, and it's different with every shore" (191) (Hurston, 1937).

FEBRUARY 24, 2009, TUESDAY, 11:36 P.M.
I moved back in with my Auntie Mel today. Last Friday, I spent the day downtown. I met Cindy Cannon, the career consultant, then I worked for a while. I spoke to Tank. He

is back in the country and out in Cali. Then I went to Imax and Martinis at the history museum with a Vanderbilt alum. Afterward, about 8:30 p.m., I got back over south, but I did not want to go home. I called my Auntie Robbin and went over there. About 11:00 p.m., her friend, Chyna, stopped by. We chopped it up quite well. She does public access television shows, and she wants me to host the youth shows. God always brings great things into your life once you decide. So, the whole time I was at Robbin's, I knew he was at home stewing. I walked in the door, and he walked out of his office, stomping and wagging the ticket from Imax, saying, "Where have you been?" I told him I was at Robbin's, but he did not believe me. He motioned as though he was going to take off his belt and whip me. He was provoking me. We started arguing. He called me a bitch and told me I was a whore. That was it. I was tired of being nervous around him and fearful he would hit me. I packed a bag and came back to Mel's house. I was so glad that was over. He was a season and gratefully a short one.

On Saturday, Auntie DeDe went to help me pack the rest of my things, but he would not let anyone in the house but me, so it took a long time. He started to realize I was leaving for good and not just a couple of days. He was extremely emotional and asked me to leave for today. I went outside and told DeDe he said I could not get anything else today. She went off, and they started arguing. She told me to call the police. The officer came, and he was talking big stuff to the officer. I got a lot more of my things, and we unpacked everything at Mel's.

On Sunday, Robbin and her guy NuNu, Mel, DeDe, and I went to see *Madea Goes to Jail.* Then I took NuNu and Tony (Mel's guy) over there to get some big things.

"This is heavy, girl," said Tony as they were moving my bookshelves into the truck.

"How much stuff do you have?" asked NuNu. They were complaining the whole time, and that made me feel horrible. I do not like inconveniencing anyone, but they were the men around me, and I did not feel comfortable going there alone. I could not lift the heavy items. We moved everything into the storage unit and then went back to Mel's house. I could not hold my emotions in. I broke down and started crying. Mel came in and said they were just playing, but it was bad taste. This may be funny to them, but this was my life, my heart, my pain. I am human. I do not share my emotions easily, but it was good to have that release.

HE called me later to apologize for his behavior. He said he knew I would not check in with him when I was out, so he could not live with me anymore. I told him his behavior was unacceptable. Since then, I have gone there Monday and today to get the rest of my things. I took him to the store both days since he does not have a car any longer. He tried to kiss me, and I said no. I told him we were breaking up because he was not honest. He knew about the baby he had on the way before he went to New Jersey. He is not a mason nor an apprentice. He did not have the money he led me to believe when we met. It's all too much. My family is done with him, anyway. They see he is controlling, and my aunts are too strong and independent to allow me to be with someone like that.

I needed that time with him to see you have to be specific about what you want. I am grateful, and he better be glad we never got physical, but we were close. God answers prayers, but not in the way you think. I asked for rest and to date a nice guy when I got to Atlanta. He was just that. That was a lesson I did not need anyone to take care of me in exchange for my independence. I now wanted a man with faith, character, and integrity. I wanted a man who can build things with his hands, a man who is fair, and a man who is not insecure and would be able to love and adore my shine, and I adore his. I wanted someone I could build a life with. I have never been afraid of hard work. Hard work is what got me through St. Ignatius, out the hood, through college, grad school, seven years in Minneapolis, and overcoming debilitating grief after my baby died.

My life became free again after that period. I made networking a priority. I was running low on funds and was looking for a job. I also started going to various churches from invites from college friends. They were PKs, or preacher's kids. I attended different types of churches, but none of them were right for me. My knowledge of the lost books of the bible was creating conflicts with the theology of the churches. Even without a church home, my faith in God was still strong. I had been obedient and moved to Atlanta. Obviously, that first relationship was not the husband God had for me.

FEBRUARY 27, 2009, FRIDAY, 10:40 A.M.

I am on a plane on my way to Chicago, but I spent this week investing in myself and developing an Atlanta network so I can find consulting opportunities. I know getting a job will not be fulfilling unless I do something where I can be creative. I am also writing and drawing again. I also want to act, which I have not done since high school.

I am starting to transcend the emotional baggage I have been carrying around for too long. My mind is open to new experiences, new possibilities, and new types of people. I am not going to limit myself or my opportunities because I have been afraid to succeed. My understanding of myself and how I deal with life has been insufficient. I am breaking through and finally loving my being in its totality. I am loving me because I finally feel ready to do what is best for me and keep healthy boundaries. I have taken a spiritual vow of celibacy to truly discover who I am and work to create who I want to be.

On Wednesday, I attended an American Institute of Architects (AIA) women's event on developing networking skills. Then yesterday, I attended the Georgia Charter School Conference. Gerard Robinson from the Black Alliance for Educational Options paid my registration. Georgia is certainly one of the most challenging states for charter schools. I am still unsure that charters are the best framework for educating Black children, since charters were created to create "White academies" as schools began to integrate (Renzulli, L., and Evans, L, 2005). African American people are known for remixing everything, so charters are just the latest version of taking something and making it work for us. It was time for me to get back into my educational advocacy work and networking.

Goals:

- Learn to draft
- Develop a three-prong model of a twenty-first-century community development center
- Pitch it to cities and counties
- Write and own a television show
- Create a line of consulting resource products
- Become an incredible and dynamic speaker

MARCH 3, 2009, WEDNESDAY, 8:30 P.M.

Yesterday, I went to the Georgia Minority Supplier Development Council orientation. The meeting was in the Suntrust building at 25 Park Place in Atlanta. It was one of my first times navigating downtown. I had been in Atlanta since July, but I was in Jonesboro, south of the city, or traveling for Fielding Nair. I attended Vanderbilt alum events in Midtown, which is where I met Patrice. I ran into her again at this meeting. I got turned around with the directions, so when I arrived the presentation had begun. I sat in the back by the door. There was a man who asked a question during the questions and answers section. He said he was an architect. I looked at him, and a whisper inside said, "That's *him!*" *That's crazy talk*, I thought, but I decided I must network with him. The guy is very fine. He looks like Tupac. He was seated across the room to my left. I kept looking in his direction, trying to get a sight of his left hand. Finally, he reached over to scratch his face, and he did not have a wedding band on. *Yes!* I thought. After the meeting, I spoke to Patrice but all the while kept my eye on him and made sure he did not leave without a proper introduction. I made my way over to him as he was speaking to another man. The man was going on and on about something I cannot recall. After what I thought was a polite enough time, I cut in and introduced myself to both.

"Hello," I said. "I am Tiffany Green. I am an education consultant, and I collaborate with architects. I heard you say you were an architect." I was super professional, but this guy looked at me in an interesting way and licked his lips.

Well, okay then, I thought.

We kept talking in the conference room until they turned the lights off. We took the elevator down to the parking level. There was a red car coming in, so we had to step back. When I stepped back, I felt my stomach drop like déjà vu. I felt like I had a memory of living this moment before. I wanted to test this gut feeling I was having, so I told him I needed to leave because I had another meeting. He asked if he could tag along.

"Of course," I said.

What I did not say was the meeting was for women entrepreneurs. We were both new to the area, so we wasted fifteen minutes following each other to the central library, which was a walking distance from where we already were. When we got to the auditorium, all the ladies doing registration were staring at him. They asked him if he knew this was a meeting for women. I played it off and grabbed my folder and stood waiting for his reaction. He laughed and looked over at me.

He said, "I'm with her." We sat inside and listened to this information about a female entrepreneurship program.

I did a similar program in Minneapolis, so I was more interested in talking to him. Plus, he was getting too much attention being one of the few men in the room. When they asked us to introduce ourselves to the people near us, we slipped out. We found a coffee shop across from Centennial Park. We talked until they closed. We did not want the evening to end, so I invited him to the house. I never do that, but I trusted him for some reason. I also knew Mel would be home soon after.

His name is Tariq Abdullah. He is thirty. He is Muslim. He is divorced with three kids (thirteen, two, and nine months). He is an architect focusing on an urban architecture program. When Mel got home, she was cool about it. I excused myself for a second and went into her room. She was like, *Who is that?* Did I mention he is handsome, six feet tall, and an Aries? I told her a little about him, and she agreed he was cute. We talked and talked all night about life, love, God, our upbringing, and past relationships.

He is on his way over here again to cook me dinner. This could be a good fit. More to come...

CHAPTER 9

T and T

———

It's amazing how you meet someone, and you know instantly they will impact your life in unbelievable ways. Tariq Abdullah is having that impact on me. Sunday, he came and picked me up. We went to Lifetime Fitness to workout. Afterward, we came back to Mel's house and had dinner. I had plans to go to Chyna's show taping. I asked him if he wanted to go. He said yes. His house was nearly an hour away, so he stayed and took a shower here and waited for me to get dressed.

We were an hour late, but we were on time because the taping was running late. It was a good show about domestic abuse. One of Chyna's friends, Angel, a pastor, asked if Tariq and I were married.

We looked at each other smiling and said, "No, we are friends."

"Well, I feel a lot of love between you both," Angel said. "When you get married, I want to sing at the wedding."

She pulled us outside to sing a song she had written. It was a beautiful song. She then asked if we had children. I said no. Tariq told her he had two who were two and nine months.

She looked at him and said, "You have to forgive her. She was wrong, and you were right."

She called us "T and T, the power couple." She told Tariq once he gets happy with me, his ex will want him back and will use his children against him. She also told Tariq I had just "cleaned house" right before meeting him, which was incredibly insightful.

Angel prayed for us. We left and went to Café Intermezzo for coffee. We talked and talked. I could see we were both trying to process what had just happened at the taping. We had a great dinner. I could not sleep after he dropped me off. He is so smart, compassionate, sexy, and chocolate.

So today, we met at Whole Foods in Midtown. I left my car, and he drove us to the Green Scene Atlanta, which is a networking event for the architecture and design community. This was a test to see how we function in that environment together. It was perfect. He went one direction once we got inside, and I went the other way. We met back two hours later, each with a stack of business cards. I was feeling the power couple vibe.

When we walked out and down the street a bit, he grabbed my hand as we turned the corner. He spun me around and kissed me so passionately. It was like a flint striking a stone. It made me think of Steve Harvey's book, *Act Like a Lady,*

Think Like a Man. I was reading the book while I was waiting on Tariq earlier that day. Men do everything for a reason. I knew that kiss was about his ease with the event and how we worked it together. We went back to Café Intermezzo for dinner. We walked around before going into the restaurant. He told me he wanted to spend quality time with me. They stay open until 2:00 a.m. It was 9:30 p.m. when we got there, and we left at 12:30 a.m. We sat outside on the patio and had more great conversation and long looks into each other's eyes. He took me back to my car in Midtown, but we sat there talking until 3:30 a.m.

I could tell there was something on his mind. I knew I needed to reassure him of my feelings. He had already explained, as a Muslim, I must "accept him" as a potential husband, so the time he spends with me is not unlawful. He told me he really liked me and wanted to fall in love, get married, and have one or two children with me. Wow, that was upfront.

MARCH 13, 2009, FRIDAY, 5:40 P.M.

The networking is bearing fruit. I followed up with a Black architect I met at Greenscene last Tuesday. He put me in contact with his boss. He is very interested in designing schools and is familiar with Fielding Nair. I am excited about the possibility of working with a Black architecture firm. I feel good about the upcoming opportunities. I also have a meeting with the Georgia Charter School Association about developing school model plans.

Tariq came over Wednesday night. We ate leftovers and watched a movie. He had to pick up his kids early, so he did not stay too late. I am starting to like him as a friend. We talk about everything.

Today I met the children for the first time. We met up at a park in Stone Mountain called Wade Walker. I stopped at a store and bought snacks and a doll for Amira. She is two and Zacharia is nine months old. Amira was very attached to Tariq, which is understandable. Zacharia came right to me. He is not walking yet. We walked around the park, and I took pictures of them. It was a sweet day. He is so caring and loving with his kids.

I am thinking about Islam and not just because of him. I have been thinking about my background, family history, prior experience in Islam, and my discomfort with Christian churches. I just cannot say Jesus Christ is my Lord and Savior when Jesus himself said do not do that or be damned. Tariq told me he wants a trustworthy, obedient Muslim wife. He said the way we get along has been like love at first sight. I want to fall, but I need more information. I told him I needed a provider and someone generous, compassionate, and trustworthy who adores me (like Barack and Michelle), passionate and supportive. I asked him, "What if I needed to travel for three weeks on business?" At first, he said that would be hard. I reminded him about where we met. We were both out, taking care of business. He loves my business mind, so being together cannot change my path but strengthen our paths together. There is so much opportunity for us. I cannot be put into a box.

Tonight, I took my Shahada with Tariq after we put the children to bed. The Shahada is the Islamic oath, one of the Five Pillars of Islam and part of the Adhan. It reads: "I bear witness that none deserves worship except God, and I bear witness that Muhammad is the messenger of God." The Shahada declares belief in the oneness (*tawhid*) of God (Allah) and the acceptance of Muhammad as God's messenger. A single honest recitation of the Shahada in Arabic is all that is required for a person to become a Muslim, according to most traditional schools.

He told me he had a vision to assist me in becoming a Muslim. I told him I wanted to become a Muslim.

He said, "If that is really what you want, you only need to recite the Shahada."

I thought about it again and said, "I'm ready."

He began to recite, *"Ashadu an la ilaha illa illa-ilah."*

I stumbled over the unfamiliar words in Arabic, *"Ashadu an la ilaha illa illa-ilah."*

He said, *"Wa ashadu anna muhammadan rasul ullah."*

I repeated, *"Wa ashadu anna muhammadan rasul ullah."*

Translation: "There is no God but God, and Muhammad is the messenger of Allah."

After saying the Shahada, he asked me to pray for him as all new Muslims have their prayers answered. I felt refreshed and excited for this new part of my life. It was a special and intimate moment. We then made Isha prayer together. I went home and took a shower. That shower reminded me of the baptism I had twenty-five years before when I was a little girl and me and Momma got baptized together. Now, as a thirty-three-year-old woman, I decided to become a Muslim. I felt like a new person.

MARCH 21, 2009, SATURDAY, 8:18 A.M.

Imagine when you become my husband
Walking to you, then hand in hand
We dance, then jet off to a distant land
Discover what Allah had planned
One woman and one man
—TIFFANY GREEN

I woke up this morning on the first day of spring renewed, rejoiced, and refreshed. Yesterday, I was emotional after speaking to my Aunt Robbin, and she told me to slow down. I asked Allah to take the salt from my mouth about reacting to my aunts' thoughts about my life. I just want them to understand I am happy. Tariq was different. He walks with a sense of dignity I had not seen before in anyone I have met or dated. He is a king, and I know I am his queen and ready for the next step to marriage.

You make me want to write
My muse, got me over the blues
Loving God, Living right
No need to fight
Just good old fashion love
The kind your read about in the Jet
Future description reads
"Married fifty years, six kids, thirteen grandkids, thirty-three
great-grandkids."
Still in love, Still in love, Still in love.
A righteous life so no strife
Friendship is the foundation
Allah made it so that March 3, 2009
Lost but found my way to you.
And we've never been apart since that fortuitous occasion
Our love grows so Deja Vu, a sign there is more than now
There was then, and there was where
Could be some ancient land
A King and Queen residing, serving, growing into Allah's
knowing
You make me
You make me
Love, Live, inspire, transgress
the material world of emptiness into
the spirit world of righteousness
You follow through
You do what you say
You love me so specially different
I love you, and I respect you
My muse.

—TIFFANY GREEN

APRIL 12, 2009

I planned a great birthday picnic for Tariq. We went to Panola State Park. I made his favorite dish of pan-seared and diced chicken with butter, salt and pepper, spinach, olive oil, mint, and finally couscous and golden raisins. He loved it. We packed up and walked through the trails taking pictures. It was one of those dates you dream about. It was a beautiful day to just frolic and play together in the woods.

APRIL 18, 2009, OUR SECRET WEDDING

My central goal in moving to Atlanta was purchasing a home. I never lived in an actual house in my life. It was always an apartment. Tariq began joining me in the home search since he knows construction and architecture. I value his thoughts. We drove around different areas in the morning, and he had a meeting at the mosque.

We prayed Dhur (afternoon prayer), and then I sat in the car as he had his meeting. He came outside and knelt by the driver's window and said, "Will you marry me?"

"Eventually," I said casually, hoping he was not serious. "One day."

"What about today?" he asked and then gave me that smile of his.

I looked away with a hidden grin, trying not to be persuaded by that smile that had melted my heart in only six weeks. He knelt there patiently without saying a word. I looked back over, wondering if he was still there.

I said, "You can't be serious. We just met six weeks ago."

"I am very serious, and I want a serious answer." He waited.

"But my family is not here. This is not my dream wedding. I mean, I have on jeans and—wait, do you even have a ring?" I asked.

He told me Imam Ihsan could marry us and his brother-in-law, Abdul Malik, can be the witness.

"I promise you a dowry of a ring and a wedding," he said, looking into my eyes lovingly, and I knew he was serious. I asked him to give me a minute. He walked assuredly into the mosque.

I sat and made a prayer. "Allah, you led me to Atlanta. You told me my husband was here. I trust in your direction. Please give me discernment." On my fingers, I quickly thought about the pros and cons of marrying him. The pros were his faith, parenting, character, integrity, intelligence, skillset in architecture, our attraction to one another, and both of us wanting and willing to build a life together. The cons were his emotionally deficient, manipulative, and abusive ex-wife and lack of present financial resources. The children were not in either bucket. I loved them and thought of gaining little children as Allah's gift for my loss of baby Oliver. Things must get better with her in a few years, I hope. They have only been apart for nine months. I can understand her being jealous and resentful when your ex marries after a divorce. My pros outweighed the cons, and I was in love with him. I decided to say yes.

Tariq and I have been married for twelve years now, and the relationship between Tariq and his ex-wife has not improved over the years. Wow, was I naive thinking things would get better? Their inability to communicate has been destructive to the children more as they have gotten older. I'm glad I couldn't see into the future because I may not have married Tariq had I known this would still be so challenging and exhausting. I focus most on protecting my peace and staying out of their relating, but I have deep compassion and concern for the children. I relate to the situation given what went down with my dad's wife, Mary, keeping him from having a relationship with me for all those years until I was an adult. It took years for my dad and me to repair our relationship, but we could never get back the time we lost. His children are teens, and the time to live with their father is slipping away.

After fifteen minutes, he came outside and began lingering near the door to the Mosque. I smiled and waved him over.

He said, "You good?"

"Yes."

"Yes, you good, or yes to my question?" he asked.

"Yes, to both," I said. His eyes lit up.

"Okay, okay, *Suphanallah!*" he said.

I never saw myself getting married like this, but as Muslims say, "Allah is the best of planners." He opened the door and went back into the mosque. There were only four of us there. Imam Ihsan married us in the Islamic tradition. He translated everything from Arabic for me. I don't remember everything. I was so nervous and excited. It was beautiful and loving. Everyone said, "Mabrook," after the ceremony. We left and went back to my aunt's house, and I cooked, and we ate. On the drive home, I told him I did not want to tell anyone we were married yet. Then we went back to his place and consummated our marriage.

JULY 2009, SHARING OUR SECRET
I attended a first-time home-buyer class and learned about a HUD program to pay for the renovations. After three months of searching for a home, we finally found the right house at the right price. It was a foreclosure. We put an offer in, and it was accepted. We selected a contractor to begin the work. The house had good bones and was well crafted but had lots of little repairs needed. Tariq's lease was up on his room, so we decided he would move with me until the house was ready.

After a few weeks, my aunts kept referring to Tariq as "my friend." I was annoyed by that because he was my husband. It was time to reveal this. We had been together nearly four months. My aunts had gotten to know him and the kids by then. I told my aunts I would cook for them on a Saturday. Right before that, I called my mother and told her Tariq and I, plus his children, would be coming for a visit.

"What's the occasion?" she asked.

I said, "He is a great person, and I want you to meet your new grandchildren."

"You are marrying him?" she asked.

"Well, he and I got married a while ago—in April, to be exact—and, well, we just wanted to let everyone in on it since we have put a down payment on a house."

She was silent just for a second and said, "You know I support you. You know what you want, and I believe he is a good person. He definitely is a good dad from what you tell me."

"He is," I said.

"Well, when are you coming? Did you tell your aunties yet?"

I replied, "I am cooking for them today, and of course, I had to tell you first. We are coming up this weekend."

"Please call your brother. You know he is going to be upset you did not tell him sooner," Momma said.

I called my brother then and told him.

After these calls, I continued making my celebratory brunch of cheesy turkey sausage quiche and a spinach salad with strawberries and pecans, and a homemade vinaigrette made of lemon juice, olive oil, salt, pepper, and honey. My three aunties, DeDe, Mel, and Robbin, arrived on time with their guys. We all ate and had small talk. Then the guys went into the screened-in porch.

As soon as they went through the door, my Auntie Robbin says, "So, what's this all about?"

Mel says, "Are you pregnant?"

"Heck no. I'm thirty-three, so trust me, I know how not to get pregnant," I said.

Then DeDe yells out, "You got married!"

I said, "Yes, we did."

They wanted all the "deets," so I began to retell our story to them, but now with all the real dates and moments they were not aware of. My Auntie Mel began to cry when I told them about the day we got married.

"I remember when you all got back that day. You were all smiley and stuff," she said.

"That is some wedding day. All you wore was jeans?" Auntie DeDe asked.

"Yep, well, when I left that day, I had not planned on getting married," I said.

"So, you all waited until you got married to... *you know*?" said Auntie Robbin.

With a side-eye, I said, "Yes."

"I guess that's why you got married so fast," said Auntie Mel.

"It was more than that, but I knew I needed to do things differently than I did them in those past relationships. You all saw what I went through with the last person, and I wanted you all to get to know Tariq before revealing this. I was also with Oliver and Tank too long, and it was ultimately a waste of my youth. I am thirty-three, and I don't want to waste any more time. Plus, Tariq would not continue seeing me without a commitment," I said.

Tariq walked into the kitchen at that moment. Auntie Mel stood up and said, "Nephew!" He walked over to the table, and all three of them gave him a hug. The guys came inside from the porch looking confused.

"What happened now?" asked Tony, Mel's guy.

"They got married a while ago," said Auntie Robbin, "and just getting around to telling us."

"Well, welcome to the family, Tar-reek," said Tony in his southern drawl and always butchering Tariq's name.

On September 9, 2009, we moved into our home. I was able to financially get us to the closing, then Tariq took over as the project manager for the renovation. The renovation was complete enough for us to move in. We did have more painting to do in the bathrooms because we needed to fire the first contractor hired to do the work. This was still a gigantic goal met. I moved to Atlanta because I wanted to buy a house. My life with Tariq was such an added blessing. All my life, I lived in apartments. No matter how long I lived in an apartment, it always felt disposable because we were only renting. No one in my immediate family owned a home. Now, we had a home of our own. A place I could put down roots. We had a large yard, four bedrooms, and three and a half bathrooms—enough room for us and the kids. We moved in with little to nothing. We both had our clothes and the books I had been carrying around for years. Before we moved in, he began working on the new back porch, which was in serious disrepair. He was a man who could fix so many things.

We had a $250 furniture budget. We saw on a list serve that a lady was having a divorce sale for bedroom furniture. We went to that home at 8:00 a.m. in the morning per the advertisement. There was one car already there. The lady came outside and told everyone to stay in their cars until she returned from dropping her children at school. The other couple's wife kept getting out of her car and going to knock on the door. The homeowner became frustrated and told them they were not welcome in. We were able to get our bedroom set with two dressers and an antique vanity for only $200. We then purchased a sofa for $25 at a secondhand shop. A family member gave us a kitchen table and chairs, so we had enough to be comfortable.

THIS STEPMOTHER THING IS NOT EASY

One of the biggest blessings and challenges in my marriage has been being a stepparent and having to deal with Tariq's ex-wife. Having lost my first child, meeting a man who is a wonderful father was supremely important to me. As soon as we married, I began trying to gel with the children. I would make sure they had the foods they needed and liked. I was conscious they have a mother, so I saw myself more as a friend and helper to Tariq. Amira was two and Zacharia was nine months when we married. They were babies, so everything was good when we were all together, but when there was any interaction with Tariq's ex-wife, Aliyyah, things became challenging.

I get it—she had young children with him, and he now remarried. I knew this would take time, and I tried to speak with her when there were pickups or drop-offs. One time, I dropped them off alone, and we had a conversation.

"*Asa Salaam Mulaikum,*" I said as I pulled up alongside her minivan at a gas station on Moreland, which was the halfway point between where we all lived.

"*Walaikum Salaam,*" she responded. We both got out of our cars. I started unbuckling Amira from her car seat. She reached for her mommy, who put her in the van, and then I handed her the car seat to buckle in her car. She got Amira settled, and we did the same dance with Zacharia.

After both children were inside, I said, "Maybe one day you and I could sit and talk. Tariq and I have been married for nine months, and I think it would be helpful if you and I could talk and separate the relationship you have with Tariq."

"We could do that," she said, "but you need to understand Tariq needs to pay child support, and he has not followed through with the things the children need."

It's 2009, and the country is still recovering from a deep recession. I responded, "Well, you have to give him time,

Aliyyah. He is working hard to create a business that lasts a lot longer than any job. The economy is coming back, and I believe he will be successful, but he needs some support. He is doing his best, but no matter what, he is an excellent father. You do see that, right?"

Her face showed she did not want to offer him any support.

I finally said, "I only offered to talk so you might get to know me. Ask me about myself since I am helping to raise your children. But if every conversation is going to be about Tariq and what he has done wrong in your opinion, then I am good. I have a lot of friends, and being friends with my husband's ex-wife is not a requirement if it only brings negativity." At that point, I gave salaams, got in my car, and drove off.

MARCH 22, 2010

My "friend," my period, has not shown up. I am excited yet nervous about possibly being pregnant. It has been six years since I lost baby Oliver. I have researched the reasons for his stillbirth, and I believe it was due to protein S deficiency. If I am pregnant, I need to start a low-dose aspirin every day and possibly be on blood thinners if my doctor prescribes it. Just to be on the safe side, I did begin the aspirin regimen. Tariq made me promise not to tell anyone until the third month. I have been sleeping a lot and not able to get anything done around the house. I took two pregnancy tests, and they were negative. It is probably too soon. I will wait until later this week to take another one.

MARCH 24, 2010

Yesterday, I resigned from my job at an architecture firm where I was the director of business development. Tariq got his first big architecture contract, and I got a consulting contract. We called this the "Geronimo plan." I have so much excitement and anxiety. It's feast or famine now. This is a new chapter in my life, and it's time to go for it. There is so much to do, and I know Tariq and I can do it all together.

Still no sign of my "friend." I am two weeks late.

APRIL 23, 2010, FRIDAY, 6:18 A.M.—CHICAGO

Tariq and I got spontaneous and decided to come to Chicago for our first anniversary. I was high strung because of my nervousness about everyone meeting him and being on my home turf. We had a little argument, and I went to visit my best friend, Anisha, alone while he stayed at the hotel for a few hours. It was great to catch up with her.

APRIL 24, 2010, SATURDAY—CHICAGO

All is well again. I do love how Tariq and I get along. We sometimes get frustrated, but we never hurt each other or take it too far. We apologize and move on. We are still getting to know each other as we have only been married one year now after only knowing each other six weeks before marrying. This year has been challenging, but our love is so deep. He is a great father, husband, friend, lover, and provider. Alfred, Anisha's husband, asked me, "Was marriage what you expected?" It is more than I expected and better because of Tariq and because we have grown a lot together. We knew who we were coming into the marriage and how to keep our communication open. And he can really fix things and build things, which qualifies him for my dream man category.

I slept all day in the hotel while he was out exploring Chicago. I finally got up about 4:00 p.m. and got dressed. He came back to the room with a gift bag. I knew he was up to something, and I do love gifts. He got me a set of bangles with a mix of yellow and white gold for our anniversary. We visited with my other best friend, Michelle, and her husband. Then we walked along Lakeshore Drive at the Promontory Point, my favorite place in Chicago.

MAY 4, 2010

The last couple of weeks have been fun and much-needed relaxation. We had a ball in Chicago. We went to a contractors' conference in Columbus, Georgia, a few days after returning to Atlanta.

I took two pregnancy tests yesterday, and they were both positive. Tariq and I went to the doctor today for an official test, but it was negative. They drew my blood for a real test, which showed low HCG. I am getting excited and anxious to know the baby is developing well and I won't miscarry. I really want this baby for Tariq and I. Tariq still does not want anyone to know.

I did tell my mother, and she said, "I knew it when you told me you were sleeping all the time!" She has a way of feeling things when it comes to us, so I was not surprised she said she knew.

This was a good weekend. My Auntie DeDe watched the kids over here so Tariq and I could tour the DeKalb Medical Center Obstetrics unit. I asked a question about the number of C-sections, and they said 35 percent of the births were cesareans. That is so high. Now Tariq and I are considering switching to a certified nurse midwife practice in the Virginia Highlands area. This practice focuses on high-risk pregnancies like mine. There are only six midwives, so I will know them when I deliver, but it will have to be at Atlanta Medical Center. They focus more on natural birth versus jumping right to surgery.

The pregnancy is going well. We have been walking every day in the park. I keep praying for a healthy baby. If induction is the best choice, I will go with it. But I really want to labor naturally without pain medicines.

I start project management training tomorrow. I was awarded a scholarship through the Workforce Investment Act through DeKalb County for $8,000 for the training. I choose a twelve-week program, since I am not working and it will get me out of the house. The program will run through mid-December. The baby is due in early January. I have been working on projects for years, so getting my project management certification will be good for my career. I am not sure when I will work again if things don't work out with this Emerson Consulting opportunity I am interviewing for.

OCTOBER 9, 2010, SATURDAY, 10:40 A.M.

I am twenty-seven weeks pregnant. I found out the sex of the baby, but I still want to surprise Tariq. It's a boy! I know how much the family needs and wants boys. My brother has four girls. I am thinking about names like Tariq, Tijjany, Tijjani, Noah, Isiah, Malaki, or something like that. It must have a meaning. I really see this boy as my future, my lineage. I love Amira and Zach, but it's not the same. I want another child to see if we can have a girl—a little mini-me. I would love to try again when the baby is one, in the spring of 2012. I will be thirty-seven then.

OCTOBER 13, 2010

I have been feeling the baby move so much the last couple of days. He feels like he is doing karate inside of me. This morning the kick took my breath away. It was so hard. I also let the cat out of the bag. I was talking about baby names. Then I messed up and said I feel like it's a boy. Tariq looked at me sternly and asked if I had found out at the ultrasound.

"Do not lie to me ever, Tiffany," he said.

I could not lie about this, so I said, "Yes, it's a boy."

At first, I think he needed a second (more like an hour) to let it sink in. When I came back from the store, he was all smiles and rubbing my stomach, saying, "You're carrying my son."

"Yes, I am," I said.

Two more weeks until the baby shower. I can't wait to see Anisha and Fallon.

OCTOBER 18, 2010, MONDAY, 3:00 P.M.

Friday, I heard back from Emerson. After three interviews and a case study, they did not hire me. I was devastated. I had the kids by myself because Tariq went to Savannah, Georgia. When he called that afternoon, I broke down on the phone. Amira was lying next to me. She was concerned, but I told her I was okay. Tariq consoled me as best as he could from a distance. It has me contemplating where I am going right now. I am going to give up on interviewing. Who is going to hire a pregnant woman?

Maybe Allah is making me be still and just focus on the baby. Last time with baby Oliver, I was working too much, and that made the baby an afterthought until I went on leave, but by then it was too late. I check on this baby all the time. If an hour goes by and I do not feel movement, I lay back and massage my stomach until the baby moves. So maybe this is my time for prayer, reflection, and just being a wife. That would be a whole lot easier if Tariq had more consistent projects. I know he is just getting the company going, but I have been independent for so long. It is hard for me to depend on anyone like this. I am going to stay positive for his sake. All I can do is depend on him.

NOVEMBER 3, 2010, WEDNESDAY, 9:30 A.M.

This past weekend was beautiful. Anisha and her daughter, Fallon, came in last Thursday. On Friday, we got the house ready for the "Cute as a Bee" baby shower. My friend, Latina, did an excellent job decorating. Chef Leroy came through with the food. It was all so good. We got a lot of gifts, but I still need a bassinet and the walker on my registry. There were many people in attendance. I wish my momma would have been here.

On Sunday, Tariq and I were lying in bed with the kids. Amira said, "Daddy, what happened? The baby didn't come at the shower."

That was precious—the mind of a three-year-old. We are coming to the end of the pregnancy. Tariq and I talked about induction. We are leaning toward it because we do not want any risk to the baby, although this might be more painful to me. I just want to make sure he comes home. We have an ultrasound today. After this week, I go to the perinatologist weekly and the midwife every two weeks.

NOVEMBER 7, 2010, SUNDAY, 2:30 P.M.
The baby is well. The perinatal doc saw calcium on his heart, which is a marker for down syndrome. He said we could get an amniocentesis to find out for sure, but there is a risk of infection, early labor. So, we decided to pass unless we needed it at thirty-six weeks to ensure his lungs were functioning. We are pretty much set on getting induced. I want natural labor, but I can't take any chances with this baby. We are thinking about the week before Christmas. My mom can come for two weeks. That will be great.

My cousin, Camilla, and her daughter, Jasmine Tiffany (named after me and we share the same birthday), have been living with us for a few weeks while she looks for an apartment. She is moving this Friday since the baby will be here soon, inshallah.

Thanksgiving was nice at the house. It was low-key; just the kids, me, Tariq, Auntie DeDe, my friend LaTina and her two kids, Auntie Robbin and her boyfriend, Camilla, Jasmine, and Auntie Mel stayed here until leaving for Nashville. They took my momma a bean pie from me.

Camilla was a big help the night before Thanksgiving. She helped me prep much of the food. I was standing too much to be so pregnant that my legs and feet swelled on Thanksgiving. I had to sit down all day with my feet up. The swelling went down the next day, but I learned my lesson.

This was my first time making a perfect bean pie. I started making them a month ago and only eating them myself or with Tariq's help. My family's oral history is that my great-great-Aunt Daisy was the creator of the bean pie. I perfected the recipe given what my mother told me was in it. I made six bean pies and three sweet potato pies, which I have been making for years. The bean pies beat them, hands down.

Tariq and I have been going back and forth about whether my mom should be in the room when I have the baby. He wants it to be just him and me. I felt very strong to have my mom, at least in the hospital. I finally told her we decided she would stay at home until the baby came. She was sad (I could tell), but she said, "I will go with your wishes." Tariq wanted that intimacy with the baby and me, and I could not deny him that right. I was nervous because of what happened with baby Oliver, but I have faith everything will be okay.

Making bean pies started this journey culminating in this book.

I am flying to Minneapolis on Sunday to do a parental involvement workshop for a charter school. The executive director is a friend, and I am so grateful to make some money right before the baby comes. I got a travel pass from my mid-wife just in case the airport gives me any problems. I need to check whether those new scanners affect the baby.

My project management class is ending tomorrow. I started six months pregnant, and now I am eight months, and I have my own special chair I can lean back in. I plan to take the certification exam in early January, but I am not sure that is realistic with the baby due on January 21.

Everything is coming to an end, and everything is beginning. I am so excited to meet my son. I am monitored weekly now, and he is doing excellent on all the tests. I could wait to go into regular labor, but I have too much anxiety about losing him like baby Oliver. I don't want to take any chances with him. The last name we came up with was Elijah Muhammad Ibn Abdullah. I wanted Elijah in front of Muhammad Abdullah, peace be upon him, because I like the name, and there are so many Muhammads.

CHAPTER 10

Growing in Love

———

The life Tariq and I began in 2009 epitomizes an old style of love where you find each other, get married (especially after six weeks), and build your life together. Often in these "modern" times, men, in particular, want to have it all and then find a wife.

It was not until I started working on this book Tariq revealed something so special about the night we went to Café Intermezzo for dinner in 2009. When we went out that night, he literally had no money in his pocket. He was on unemployment at the time, and he knew at midnight his unemployment would be direct deposited into his account. That is why he delayed going into the restaurant. We took our time, and the check came at 12:15 a.m. I never knew anything about it. We fell in love over that meal. His faith was a cloud that floated him right into my heart.

Tariq was God's promise to me. God told me in 2008 to move to Atlanta and that my husband was there. I was obedient, and my faith moved me here with my aunties. I had overcome so much in Minneapolis with my baby Oliver being stillborn in 2004. The bone-crushing grief and depression was debilitating. I never thought I would escape it. There were times in Minneapolis where suicide seemed like the best choice, but God saved me and created me to be a Muslim, gave me a righteous and loving husband, and prepared me for motherhood with Tariq's children in preparation for my own son and the beginning of our life together. This time would build my faith, family, and my fortitude.

DECEMBER 16, 2010, THURSDAY, 5:15 A.M.

I woke up at 3:45 a.m. with Braxton-Hicks contractions. I have had them off and on for a week. I have a midwife appointment this evening to check if my cervix has dilated any. At my last appointment, the midwife went through different options for being induced. I wanted to go full term, but I am getting too anxious about losing the baby. My mom gets here on Saturday. I am looking forward to having her here for two weeks. It is getting harder for me to move around, so she can help me cook, and just having her here will make me calmer.

DECEMBER 21, 2010, TUESDAY, 10:10 P.M.

The birth story began on Friday, December 17, when we went into the perinatologist for an amniocentesis to ensure the baby's lungs were mature for the induction scheduled to start on December 20. My amniotic fluid was low, so Dr. Jacobsen told me to go into the hospital at once for an induction. Tariq and I went back home to pack, and we got to Atlanta Medical Center about 5:00 p.m. They gave me Cytotec to start the contractions at 9:00 p.m. The contractions started but fizzled out by the next morning. Then I got two more induction medicines, Cervidil and Pitocin, but still not much happened. The team ramped things up with the foley catheter, which was a long, rubber tube with an inflatable balloon on one end that the doctor fills with air or sterile water. Then they gave me more Pitocin.

I was in bed from Friday, so by Sunday afternoon, I was lethargic and starving. Can you believe they did all that for two days and expected me to push out a baby without food? They wanted to break my water, so I begged them for a break so I could eat and take a shower. I felt so much better afterward. I knew it was time to have this baby. If Monday morning came without a baby, the doctors were going to slice and dice me with a C-section. I was not having that. The midwife, Dr. Jan, wanted to put in an internal monitor to get better stats on the baby. It would also get more fluid to the baby if necessary. But this was right as the shifts were changing.

Sallie, the certified nurse midwife, broke my water and said I did not need the internal monitor. Tariq got upset because she did not mention this before breaking my water. So, we went without them for a while longer. I had strong contractions, but the baby went flat in terms of activity. After three hours, the nurse came in and said she wanted me to move around because she did not like to see the monitor flat. She wanted to see the baby monitor with more highs and lows. Tariq was again concerned about not having the internal monitors and why they were not supplying more fluid to cushion the baby when I was already low on fluid.

The midwife came in and asked Tariq why he was so concerned and went on about how she knew more about this. I was sitting on the edge of the bed with strong (6/10) contractions. I yelled at Tariq and asked him to relax, but I was really getting nervous. He told me today, when I went to the bathroom, he took the staff in the hall and demanded Sallie put the monitor in. The baby had not been flat for three days until she broke my water. She begrudgingly put it in and saw I was four centimeters dilated. They added more fluid, and within an hour, I was seven centimeters. An hour later, I was ready to push.

This goes to show the importance of having an advocate, either a family member or a doula, there for the mother, especially a Black mother. I had already lost one baby, and my husband made sure we would not lose this baby.

At 1:08 a.m., I delivered a six-pound, five-ounce baby boy. He is beautiful. Tariq named him Muhammad Ibn Abdullah after the prophet, PBUH (peace be upon him).

As soon as the baby arrived, Tariq recited the adhan (the Islamic call to prayer) in one ear and said a prayer in the baby's other ear. I cried so hard. I could not believe he was here and healthy. I longed for him since the day I lost baby Oliver. I would never let myself daydream about him until he was here in my arms. It has been a long road since 2004.

I cannot say enough about Tariq. He was an incredible coach. I would not have been able to go through the induction without pain medicines without him. He coached my breathing through every single contraction. I would be hot during the contraction, and he would ice my forehead and back. In between, I would be freezing cold and needed a warm blanket. We went through this hot and cold dance for three hours before I squatted and pushed the baby out.

Tariq was my hero, and I was his warrior woman. He has not left my side, and this experience has truly bonded us and let me know Allah guided me to the right partner. Tariq is my best advocate. I need to honor him better and not fight him so much on things he wants to do and wants for me. That's why I said okay to the name he wanted. He deserved it for everything he did for us. I am so glad we entered this journey together. I cannot wait for everyone to meet Muhammad and watch him grow up. He's going to be special. I can feel it.

JANUARY 5, 2011, WEDNESDAY, 8:36 P.M.

The baby is sleeping in his bassinet. I am concerned about him. He's eating intermittently and did not sleep well last night. He has a hernia and may need surgery if it does not close. I have some food allergies and Dr. Askari, a naturopathic doctor in our Islamic community, prescribed some tonics. I have been keeping a food journal for two weeks. It could be why I've had so many yeast infections and why I'm now staying off sugar, dairy, carbs, and all things white. I'm not breastfeeding until I am better.

The Islamic Conference Tariq is coordinating is almost here. I get my husband back again. He is burning himself out with all these late-night calls.

JANUARY 12, 2011, WEDNESDAY, 10:00 P.M.

The last couple of days have been rough. I am exhausted, nervous, on edge, and irritable, all from lack of sleep. I have not had more than two hours of sleep at a time since Muhammad was born. Zach and Amira are still here. The weather took a turn, and we have been iced in since Sunday. Tariq was able to go out yesterday for groceries.

I am bonding well with Muhammad. I have been sad and frustrated when he cries so much and I can't stop him. I have had some blue thoughts, but I love my little man. He is wonderfully beautiful, a perfect blend of Tariq and me. He's healthy but has been congested. I have the humidifier on and have given him saline drops. He is spitting it up well. Hopefully, he will be well soon. The kids want to be around him, but I am quite overprotective right now because he is so new.

The Islamic conference is this weekend. Tariq's sister, Nurah, flew in tonight. She asked me now that I've bonded with Ibn what I think about putting him in daycare. That was a bad question to ask me. My response was short.

"I haven't thought about any of that." She changed the subject, but a red flag went off about her. This was only our second meeting, with the first time in Detroit on our visit this summer, so we don't know each other well. I will have to watch her.

JANUARY 30, 2011, SUNDAY, 9:00 P.M.

Yesterday was my thirty-fifth birthday. Wow. What a blessing. I don't feel that age but rather twenty-three to twenty-five years old. I always say that. Tariq and I took Ibn to Auntie DeDe's house to stay with her for the night. Then we went on a date to the movies and Barnes & Noble, where we talked and read. Tariq wanted to go bowling or play pool, but I was tired. I almost fell asleep in the movie. We saw *True Grit*. It was nice spending the day with Tariq. He has been working on an Islamic conference for the last few months, and I am so glad it was a success. Tariq gave me a watch and white gold earrings for my birthday. He is great at gift-giving. We also stopped by the Sheraton, where Camilla gave Jasmine Tiffany her thirteenth birthday sleep-over.

Anisa, Tariq's mom, had a stroke a few days ago. I am making dua every prayer for her. I will go and pick up Ibn later today. I called DeDe, and he is doing fine. I needed some rest. Alhamdulillah.

Catching back up a couple of weeks, the conference was a great success. It was well run and attended. I am proud of Tariq's involvement. Me and Ibn went on Friday to support Tariq. It was hard getting there. It was my first real outing with the baby. I melted down in the car because I was tired and anxious. I was only a three-week mother. Tariq came outside and kissed me. I appreciated that. I did not stay and went back home and went back to sleep. We went back on Saturday for a little while. Then I went to Auntie Mel's house to visit with her.

FEBRUARY 11, 2011, 5:48 A.M.

I have been up with Ibn since 4:15 a.m. I started him on the homemade organic rice formula prescribed by Dr. Billiot, a naturopathic doctor in Marietta, Georgia, and referred by Dr. Askari last night. He also had acupressure yesterday to get rid of his fungi and gas caused by the soy formula. By the time we got home, he was cooing and expressive. We spent yesterday buying everything for the formula and getting organized. His first feeding was midnight. It's a lot thicker than the soy formula and so much healthier. He is doing better. He is in his bassinet calling me, but I'm in the bathroom, my preferred place for journaling. My mom gave me some good advice with the children. She said, "Just love on them and show them attention and affection."

FEBRUARY 16, 2011, WEDNESDAY, 10:45 A.M.
I decided to keep applying for jobs to become independent again. If something hits, then I will go for it, but until then, I am home with my boy. I am going to try harder with the kids this weekend. I will try to take my mother's advice and shower them with affection and see what happens.

MARCH 16, 2011, WEDNESDAY, 8:00 A.M.
We still haven't seen Zach and Amira since February 25.

APRIL 16, 2011, SATURDAY, 10:10 A.M.
Last night, Tariq, Ibn, and I went to the Imperial Fez Moroccan Restaurant. It was a great time and sort of a pre-anniversary. The owner is Tariq's new client. I ask Allah to help him get this project; to help me be a better mother; to help me increase my deen. My faith is growing, and so is my knowledge. Eventually, I would like to give dawah (outreach about

Islam) to women in prison. I'm still not sure what I should be doing right now, but I know Allah has a plan why I have no plan. Next week I am going to put some time into Tarchitects (Tariq's architecture firm), Inshallah, and really help Tariq. It's time to find my lane in the community.

APRIL 17, 2011, MONDAY, 12:25 A.M.

Today was a great day. I attended the Sisters Town Hall Meeting at Atlanta Masjid of Al-Islam. I spoke out about the difficulty of meeting sisters and developing friendships as a new Muslim. Many sisters had the same concerns. I offered to administer a Meetup.com group. The masjid will support it financially. I met many great sisters, including Imam Mansur's wife, Fatimah. She was nice. I am feeling a lot better about being a part of the community.

Sign up flyer in 2012 for Sisters to Sisters of Al-Islam.

I created Sisters to Sisters of Al-Islam from July 2011 to 2013, sponsored by Atlanta Masjid. We held thirty events over the two years of the meetup. That group filled a critical void in my community life and established my leadership in the Atlanta Black Islamic community. We held events in my home, but as we grew, we met at restaurants, did social activities, and volunteered during Ramadan for Iftars at the Masjid. I met some of my closest friends, Aseelah, Zakiyyah, Shaherrah, Carmen, Latonya, and many other women through Sisters to Sisters. Our children have grown up together. I have watched my younger sisters get married and have families. I thank

Allah for that opportunity and the leadership to create the group, not just what it provided me but for what it gave so many sisters I met. As my career started again, I could not keep the group going, so I closed the meetup in 2013.

APRIL 20, 2011

The situation with the children is escalating. Aliyyah is not budging, and it is really making everything difficult. We were supposed to meet this morning, but she canceled the meeting last night. We still have not seen the children since February.

MAY 20, 2011, FRIDAY, 8:30 A.M.

Today Ibn makes five months. He is such a happy baby. He is always laughing and smiling. He's so big now—seventeen pounds and 25.5 inches. I am thinking about entering him in baby contests. His teeth should start to come in soon. He is already in size six to nine-month clothing.

I am really fascinated by hijab fashion. I have been buying more scarves and wearing them in more styles as well as researching hijab websites around the world. I found some high fashion sites that inspire my wardrobe. I also watch out for certain sisters at mosque who have a certain effortlessness about their hijab that is so impressive. I love it when it looks like hair. It just flows and you don't see pins anywhere. I don't know how they do it. I have learned to get up early on Friday to work on my hijab or even prework my hijab a day or so before and take pictures because it can take me two or three hours before it feels comfortable without me poking myself.

Also, next week Tariq and I have a meeting with Aliyyah and all the imams to meditate about the children. It will be good to see the kids soon.

JUNE 8, 2011, WEDNESDAY, 11:40 A.M.

Hooray! The kids are back. They have been here a week. The Imam awarded Tariq a full thirty days, June 1–June 30, to make up for the ten days times three visitations we missed. Tariq has to pay back child support. I got Aliyyah to agree to pay toward NAET treatments for Zacharia because that poor baby is suffering so bad from food allergies. Nambudripad's Allergy Elimination Techniques, also known as NAET, are a noninvasive, drug-free, natural solution to alleviate allergies of all types and intensities using a blend of selective energy balancing, testing, and treatment procedures from acupuncture/acupressure, allopathy, chiropractic, nutritional, and kinesiological disciplines of medicine. His hands especially, around his mouth, legs, and inside his elbow are all scabbed up from eczema. We will start that next week, hopefully, inshallah.

Aliyyah and I were cordial, although I held my ground when needed. I was the one who got all of us to a win-win. Tariq was being stubborn and was about to lose the war over a battle, so I stepped in and gave Aliyyah her one hour per Sunday over the month they are here. Maybe that will give us a chance to get to know one another. I have never been against getting to know her, but she tries to manipulate the situation and use the moment to talk shit about Tariq, and I won't have that. Only time will tell.

Tariq and I are actively trying for another baby. I want one more, and then our family will be complete. Maybe Allah will bless me with a girl or twins. I know Tariq is nervous about me being pregnant again, but inshallah we will have a beautiful outcome like Ibn. He is such a special baby. I don't have all the allergies anymore, and I know what to do to breastfeed as well as supplement with homemade formula, the supplement tubes, and to take fenugreek early, early. I need to start taking my prenatal again.

JUNE 11, 2011, SATURDAY, 8:39 A.M.

The house is quiet for now, with enough time to hopefully write, use the bathroom, and take a shower before going downstairs to make breakfast. All the kids are asleep except Amira. She is quite the big sister. She is very helpful, obedient, and a good little girl. There has been a great turnaround since last year. She is not whining anymore since she has been home. Zach is becoming a big boy.

I came on my period on Thursday, so no baby yet. It was just nice to think about another baby, but I really need to make some income and get my finances in order ASAP. Maybe in a year or so, we will try again. I need to get TGC—Tiffany Green Consulting—more active again now that Ibn is getting bigger. It's time for me to get back out into the world and start networking again. I miss the old me sometimes.

JUNE 17, 2011, FRIDAY, 2:00 A.M.

Tariq and I got home about 1:30 a.m. from a great date night. We first went to the Atlanta Central Library for a book signing with Sista Souljah then a discussion about her book, *Midnite*. It was really inspiring and has me wanting to write. Writing seems a great fit for my lifestyle and the mix of empowerment, teaching, and business skills I want to share. Then we went to Tantra for dinner. The food was great. Afterward, we went to our favorite Café Intermezzo for dessert and played chess on Tariq's tablet. It was so nice to get out and have some alone time. Tariq's brother, Mansur, kept the kids. He's been staying with us for nearly a month.

JULY 15, 2011
Yesterday Mansur's wife, Jenn Layla, came to get him from Virginia. She stayed overnight then they left. He seemed better than when he came. I got to know him better over the six weeks he was here. I wish him the best and them the best.

In May 2021, for Eid (the Islamic holiday at the end of Ramadan), Tariq, Muhammad, and I traveled to Virginia to visit his Abu (dad). We shared an Airbnb with Mansur and Jenn Layla with their two sons, Amir and Zayd. They are also expecting their third child later in 2021. I am proud of their marriage, and even though it was a tough time for them and for us as a family, we helped each other out and have grown as a family. Alhamdulillah.

JULY 23, 2011, SATURDAY, 11:00 P.M.
I saw on Facebook my cousin Jessica got engaged. I am happy for her and know she'll have an exquisite wedding.

Then I started feeling blue about the special and traditional moments I had foregone because we didn't have them or because I did things in nontraditional ways. I married Tariq after six weeks and did not get everything I really wanted. Tariq says we can have a wedding, but I want it right, the way I see it in my mind. I want to have it at the house, but I want our landscape impeccable. I inadvertently snapped a bit at Tariq about the upkeep outside. I framed it by saying how he probably wouldn't like it if I didn't wash clothes for weeks or let the dishes pile up. I apologized, but there is a foot of grass in the backyard and leaves and branches everywhere. I want to be all beautiful and share in our love with everyone. For once, I want to do things properly.

Another issue is resenting my loneliness. I feel very isolated. I love my little family, but for so long, I was free and independent. I miss that sometimes—a lot, actually. I don't get to go out. I know I always wanted marriage and kids, but I think about my life in twenty years when they are all grown up. Converting to Islam has been a blessing, but it took a bit of carefreeness from my life. I don't know if it's good or bad. I was never a bad person. I was pretty modest. Of course, no alcohol or drugs have been great for my mental stability and recurring depression. Sometimes I just don't want to think so hard about my attire and being covered.

SEPTEMBER 8, 2011, THURSDAY, 11:15 P.M.
Today I went down to a Wells Fargo Home Mortgage Workshop. I'm trying to get a loan modification. I have to send some additional paperwork in for our income, but hopefully we'll get a reduction. I am down to the last $1,500 of my

pension. I have been using it over time to pay bills as a last resort. I am nervous about the next couple of months. I am applying for jobs. I'll take an executive assistant position if I have to.

We haven't seen the kids again since August 20. Tariq is so upset, but his mother, Anisa (Umm), is here, seeing Dr. Askari. She has been a good distraction, but she also wants to see her grandchildren.

SEPTEMBER 28, 2011, WEDNESDAY, 1:35 A.M.
I just finished changing Ibn again. He's had diarrhea since Sunday. That's been hard with the cloth diapers, but I just keep washing them. We are going to the doctor today to make sure it's nothing serious. He's strong, though, and still active. Well, 75 percent, but that's a lot for him.

I have a great idea for his first birthday party. It's going to be a costume theme. Muslim children don't do Halloween, so if I get invites out soon, or a save the date, people can buy a costume or keep the Halloween one if they're not Muslim. I need to come up with an invite list. I will pull out the baby shower list and Muslimahs with small children.

SEPTEMBER 30, 2011, FRIDAY, 7:00 A.M.
Muhammad still has diarrhea. Dr. Askari said it's not a virus or bacteria, but the probiotics in his formula are too strong. She still didn't tell me how many days before it would get better.

Tomorrow is the Sisters to Sisters Sushi Sister outing. I need to plan an agenda today. It should be fun.

OCTOBER 3, 2011, MONDAY, 10:00 A.M.

Sushi Sisters was fabulous. Seven people came, including me. We really had a great time. RuSans is cheap and good. One of the members, Zakkiyah, brought her sister, Shaheerah. She has kids around the same age as Muhammad, Zach, and Amira. We will schedule a playdate, and I want her to come to the birthday party. She seems nice, a little reserved, though.

Umm is still here. She's almost ready to go home. I hope Tariq will take her to her doctor's appointment. We are really in a bad way financially. If one of us doesn't get a job or project soon, we're at risk of losing the house. We would be homeless because there is no place else for us to go. I'm really scared now.

OCTOBER 7, 2011, FRIDAY, 10:00 A.M.

Ibn is on day twelve of diarrhea. It is a little bit less, and I have added more rice to his formula and cut out the probiotics. He is still active. He has another doctor's appointment this week. I may see if he can be seen on Monday when Umm goes in.

My "friend" is here on time this month. Thank God. We have decided not to have another baby anytime soon. I'm very happy with that decision because there are too many stressors happening right now. I need to get my career moving and gain financial stability and health insurance. I would prefer to try again before I turn forty.

OCTOBER 9, 2011, SUNDAY, 9:00 A.M.

I was listening to Tariq's Millionaire Mindset, and I realized I had lost the confidence that has gotten me so far in my life. If I am going to do any one of my many business ideas, I have to focus and have confidence and persistence. I am starting Oprah's Life class tomorrow. I really need inspiration and education. I am ready to move into a new phase—mommy with it all.

I do have it—or at least the potential to have it all. I spoke with Randy at Fielding Nair to discuss the consulting opportunity I could not complete because of needing to take care of the children. I told him I could have it all, but not all at the same time. But maybe I can, just not the way I think. I have the time now. When Tariq gets another project, things will get easier, but I can't just wait around. I can't make excuses that I have a baby, I don't have any money, etc. So many people create successful businesses with nothing but confidence, drive, persistence, and a little money. So, I do what I want to do...

- Create a fashion magazine for the modest modern woman
- Find a full-time job using project management skills in education, higher education
- Market my education planning skills to architecture firms

OCTOBER 15, 2011, SATURDAY, 9:00 A.M.

My paternal grandmother, Sadie Sharks Cantrell, passed away Thursday night. I am sad we were not able to get back to Wynne, Arkansas, this summer. I only met her once in 1996 when I went to Memphis to visit Auntie Debbie. I met my grandfather, who was in the hospital, my grandmother, and my cousin, Keisha. My Auntie Debbie thought Keisha was me because we looked so much alike. I had a lot of resentment back then after I met them that time. I felt like I had missed out on so much. I regret not seeing them more. The funeral is next weekend. I may have to go without Tariq, or he will come later, because the National Organization of Minority Architects conference is in Atlanta and he is speaking.

OCTOBER 20, 2011, THURSDAY, 7:15 A.M.
Today Tariq is speaking at the NOMA conference. I wish I could be there to see his presentation. I'm sure he will do well. He is speaking at the architect's response to the social dilapidation of US cities. We could not afford for me to go to my grandmother's funeral. My dad understood.

OCTOBER 26, 2011, WEDNESDAY, 12:50 A.M.
I had sewing class today at the masjid on the west end. I think we need more structure and someone to watch the children. I am working on a skirt.

I have a phone interview on Friday with Georgia State University Project Management Office. I'm excited. I want to work in higher education. I love the learning environment, and GSU seems like a great urban school and may open some opportunities to teach and get my PhD. I need to start reviewing my PMP information so I can take the exam before the year is out.

NOVEMBER 4, 2011, FRIDAY, 1:26 A.M.

Just fed and put Ibn on the toilet. He's doing well using the bathroom. Hopefully, he will be trained before he can say "potty."

Good news, I am one of the two finalists for the project manager position at Georgia State University. I really want this and need this. I ask Allah to make it mine! We need it bad financially, and it would be a great step in my career. It's a learning environment that's innovative and needs my skill set. The team seems great. I like everyone and really want to get to know them.

Umm went back to Detroit. She is better alhamdulillah. I wish I had known upfront she was going to be here for two and a half months. To get her home, Tariq had to use his debit card, which is now negative because no one would pitch in for the ticket. But Allah has us.

NOVEMBER 11, 2011, FRIDAY, 11:11 P.M.

This time will never happen again in my lifetime. And the day was full. Jummah at Masjid Mu-mineen on Hank Aaron, then picking up Zach and Amira, then going to Mamie's in Marietta to order cupcakes for Muhammad's party, then to Tadpoles for Eid gifts (toys and clothes) then out to eat at Ilforno's on Roswell Road. When we got back in, I made Ibn formula while Tariq played with him before bed.

And great news...

I got the job at Georgia State University as a project manager.

This is a new career. This is my first official project management position. I am excited and just happy. I will be earning a living again. I was also blessed to find a great Muslim daycare right near the house. She is the wife of an imam. She is $100 per week. Tariq can take him when he wants. It will be the same price for Zach and Amira when they are here.

It is such a blessing to have this job. The team is good. I can get my PhD paid for as well as professional development. All is looking up.

DECEMBER 4, 2011, SUNDAY, NOON
I finished my first week at GSU. Observations:

Very casual environment as far as dress. Good home-life balance possibility. Janice, my boss, is easygoing and wants me to succeed. I like Eboni, my coworker. She has been there a few years.

Next week I am going to sit down with as many managers as possible so I can get to know them and vice versa.

Muhammad started daycare. He does well. I wish I could stop in on him, but he's happy when he comes home. He went three days last week. Maybe two days this week because he has a cold. Tariq has been a little down this week. I think it's because he wants a full-time job. He redid his cover letter and résumé. He's applying for a yearlong Loeb Fellowship program for architects at Harvard. I will be a single mom for a year if he goes. It will be great for his career. That's going to be hard but worth it.

Today is Muhammad's first birthday. It is amazing to see him growing up so fast. He is becoming independent. He is very determined and curious. He likes to find out how things work. Sometimes he is clingy, but I think we balance showing him attention to encourage his independence. I can do better at spending time doing things together. We do need to remove the pacifier from the equation. We have become lazy about it, and he expects it. We need to use it for sleep only and then on a weekend remove it all together.

Tariq and I are okay. The last six to nine months have been challenging with a new baby and having his brother here six weeks and his mom here two and a half months. I loved getting to know Mom, but having just had a baby, it was all a lot for me. They were pulling on us financially, and we have still not recovered. I am frustrated by all this. I am always trying to save everyone and doing too much. I need to see Tariq make it happen for this family. I am working now, but it's not enough. He needs to get all the money owed to him from family and projects and start us off right in 2012.

DECEMBER 23, 2011, FRIDAY, 8:50 A.M.

Sitting in the kitchen feeding Muhammad. He's eating Japanese sweet potatoes with ground chicken and carrots. He's doing good with the table food. Dr. Askari wants us to transition him off the rice formula because it is blocking his adrenal system. He had an appointment yesterday. He is twenty-four pounds, eight ounces, thirty-one inches, with a forty-nine centimeter circumference head. That put him in the ninetieth percentiles for height and seventy-fifth percentiles for weight. He is good other than his small intestine and food blockages. I can't believe my little baby is one year old. He is such a happy baby. Mashallah.

DECEMBER 25, 2011, SUNDAY, 8:40 P.M.

Today is Christmas. Tariq and I are establishing a yearly tradition of cleaning out the garage on Xmas and posting things to free cycle or sitting them outside. The garage looks great. There is so much room now, and we were able to get rid of a lot of junk and baby items we don't need anymore. My aunties are keeping Muhammad for New Year's Eve. I am looking forward to having some alone time with Tariq. I am planning a spa night in. I want to rekindle the flame and put behind us the stress of 2011 and move into 2012 happily married. Tariq is wonderful in so many ways. I want so much to be in love the way I was in the beginning, but life, stress, etc., has gotten in the way.

The lack of consistency in our finances has me in a tizzy. I don't want to verbally vomit all over him with all my thoughts, so I have to express myself here and think it all out. The other night he declared he did not want any more children. I am still processing whether that is a deal breaker for me. I want at least one more child.

There is more to a relationship than just love. I love him, but his other children, his other responsibilities—it may be too much for him to keep up with that and this family. I am trying to be patient. I have invested so much already, and now we have a child together. I have to think about Muhammad and me. I just spoke to Vikki for a long while, and that was helpful. She said 2012 is going to be pivotal for me. She is right. I will give it more time and try to help Tariq more. Or rather, give him more time to work his issues out. We should know more about Harvard in March.

Tariq did not get accepted into the Harvard program but got a position at another architecture firm in town in early 2012. Our friendship has been a consistent foundation in our marriage. When we get into a tough place, we use a technique I coined "friend zone." When I need to say something difficult, I will say, "Can I talk to you just as your friend?" He usually gives me a positive reaction, and it lowers his defenses.

Marriage is not easy. You must work at it every day. I mean, every day. There are no vacations in marriage. I think that is called divorce. He and I have had a lot of rough times over the now twelve and a half years we have been married, but we always find our way back to each other through a conversation about how we met or looking at photos of the children when they were little. We would have some tougher times ahead.

CHAPTER 11

Growing in Faith

———

JULY 5, 2012, 1:30 A.M.

I just got back from Chicago on Monday. I was the matron of honor at my best friend Michelle's wedding. The wedding party was huge. I think it was twenty between the bridesmaids and groomsmen. We danced and partied all night. I have been feeling down since I got back. Over the five days in Chicago, I saw a glimpse of my old self. She is funny, crazy, spontaneous… I missed her, and I need her back. I lost myself trying to be a wife, a mother, a Muslim, and a professional. Can I really be myself and be with Tariq? I used to think I could, but maybe I was trying to make me work for him and fit what he wanted. I gave up habits, and I don't want them back, but some things are just too serious. And losing myself is the most serious. I am trying to be everything for everybody and not myself. I don't want to lose Tariq. He's been a good man to me and a great father to our baby. I don't want Muhammad to go through what all Tariq's other children are going through, with parents not getting along. Also, last night, he told me if he ever wanted someone else, he would tell me if it made sense. And he wonders why I feel down.

I want a legal marriage because of our son. He deserves more than an easy in and easy out Muslim marriage. I don't even remember what we said when we got married. We had no nikah, no paperwork, not even a ring at the time. I'm not trying to diminish saying our vows before Allah, but if I don't remember what we said, does it really count? I don't know what tomorrow brings other than I need to take *much better care of myself so* I don't feel so insecure and angry.

In between the periods of not journaling, my life as a married woman and mother were becoming more intense. I was finding less and less time for myself.

JANUARY 21, 2013, MONDAY, 11:53 P.M.
Wow. I can't believe I have not written in my journal since July 2012. It was hidden under a curtain by my bedside table. That's sad, so let me catch you up.

The marriage issue has a resolution. Tariq and I got legally married on November 9, 2012. We went to the courthouse in DeKalb County, Georgia.

Muhammad turned two in December. My dad stayed with us for six days for Muhammad's party. That was the first time since I was three years old that I was with my dad overnight. He was a great house guest. He cleaned the yard and helped Tariq clean the garage as part of our Christmas tradition.

Dad and Muhammad hit it off. Muhammad loves his "paw-paw." He needs my dad in his life. There are so few men in our family who can play an active role. I can't wait until he comes back. He lives back in his hometown of Wynne, Arkansas, and he is caring for his dad, my grandfather, who is 103-year-old. We were able to have some much-needed conversations about the past and why he has been gone for so long. He apologized for all the pain his relationship with Mary caused my mother and me. He regretted marrying Mary. He wished he would have married my mother. That was healing to know and hear, but those years are gone. I asked him to just be a great grandfather to Muhammad. The memories he makes with him are the most important thing to me now.

Work is cool. I passed my project management professional (PMP) certification exam in October. I am looking for a director level positions now. I know I can do so much more and make more money.

In October, I had an ectopic pregnancy. I was eight weeks pregnant. I had emergency surgery. They saved my tubes. I wish I had them tie them. I refuse to get on any birth control. I have been on birth control off and on since I was fifteen. If Tariq doesn't want children, he will need to do something about it. I am thirty-six, and I can't take any more hormones.

Sisters to Sisters has eighty-seven members now. I am always thinking about how to engage members better. We need a strategic plan and curriculum for the members. Maybe a retreat in June before Ramadan. I still feel different from the other sisters. I am my own person and feel comfortable being me. I am not judging them, but I sometimes feel from the conversations they want to be freer, but they don't have the license and independence to live their lives the way they want. I love Allah, and he knows my heart, enough said. I don't wear hijab 90 percent of the time any longer. Sometimes I feel self-conscious with it, and sometimes I feel self-conscious without it. When I'm in different settings, I decide whether to wear it or not.

My birthday is coming up. I am having a couples' dinner at Thrive on February 2. Hopefully, it will be nice. Mom just had her sixtieth birthday. Tariq, Muhammad, and I drove to Nashville. We surprised her with a brunch. She cried. I was so glad to see her happy and healthy at sixty. Amen!

JUNE 21, 2013, FRIDAY, 7:17 A.M.
Okay, now it has been six months since I last journaled. Catch up time. I had a wonderful birthday dinner with four couples.

And drum roll...

I found out on June 15 I am pregnant. Yes, pregnant! Tariq was against having a baby for the last two years but changed his mind a few months ago when he saw the impact of Amira and Zach leaving every other weekend was having on Muhammad. I knew all along this would create difficulty for little man. When they leave, they have one another, but Muhammad is left alone. God willing, everything will be fine with the pregnancy, financially and health wise for me.

In May, I started a new fitness routine. I have lost five pounds since then. I have lost some inches. My intentions are to continue lifting weights and go hard this pregnancy, or at least as hard as I can. I only want to gain ten pounds and the rest be all baby. I see the midwife, Marsha Ford, on Monday. Because of being older and high-risk, she was recommended to me. I am so happy Tariq came around. I had wanted to wait a few months, but it was too late. I am already pregnant (PG).

JUNE 25, 2013, TUESDAY, 11:45 P.M.
Mom came to Atlanta on Thursday, and she left today. It is always good spending time with her. Tariq and I told her we were pregnant. She is excited. We are not telling anyone else, although I did tell Michelle and Vikki. They are my besties. The due date is February 19, 2014. This weekend we took family pictures. They came out nice. The rest of the time, we just chilled. Tariq and I are in a great place.

AUGUST 30, 2013, FRIDAY, 10 P.M.—POSITIVE T21 TEST
Things were going well with the PG until two days ago. I took a test called a Materniti21 that tests for chromosomal abnormalities. It's a blood test to test fetal DNA through my blood. I didn't think twice about the test until I got a call from the perinatologist's office about the results. I was sitting in my cube at Georgia State University.

"Is this Mrs. Green-Abdullah?" the doctor asked.

"Yes, this is she," I said.

"Did anyone call you about the results of your T21 tests? Your positive test results, I mean," he said.

"One second, please, let me go into a conference room," I said as I got up and walked around the corner into a small room.

I could feel my ears burning and my chest heaving as I was trying to process what he just blurted out. "Now, what are you saying? No one has called me except you. You said it is positive. What—what does that mean?"

He replied in a robotic tone. "Mrs. Green-Abdullah, you took a T21 test because of your geriatric age of this pregnancy, and a positive result means this fetus may have trisomy twenty-one or down syndrome. Are you considering terminating the pregnancy?"

"Excuse me! Sir. You just said a lot, and then you asked me if I was going to end the pregnancy. Is it standard for that information to come with that question?" Tears rolled down my eyes. I felt like he knocked the wind out of me. "I need to talk to my husband. Is there someone else who we can talk to?" I asked.

He said, "Yes, you can call the office and schedule an appointment when you feel up to it."

I hung up and sat in shock for a minute and then called Tariq. I told him what the doctor said and that "I didn't want to have a baby with down syndrome (DS)."

He told me to relax and "everything will be okay." I went home, and we tried to schedule a consult and amniocentesis for the next day, but I was only fourteen weeks, so it was a week too early. We asked them not to schedule us ever again with the doctor who called me, and he explained why. The receptionist understood his concerns and scheduled us with an African American woman doctor who was sympathetic and answered all our questions.

She also informed us about the racial component of potentially having a child with down syndrome. She said 95 percent of African American down syndrome pregnancies are terminated for various reasons but mostly due to economic, social, and cultural stigma. She said the doctor who called was out of line and insensitive. He was used to most Black patients terminating. She put Tariq and I at ease. She also recommended we go to Emory and get a consult from the gene therapy center to get a better understanding of down syndrome.

The next day, I asked Tariq about our Islamic options. He said when he was in Senegal, the sheikh taught him the soul does not enter the baby until 120 days. Today we are day one hundred. We have twenty days to have the amniocentesis, get informed about DS, get the results, and decide whether to keep the baby or terminate and get that procedure done.

On days one and two, I was terrified and could not see a life for this baby being anything but unknown, painful, and hard. After talking to someone with a DS kid, researching on the internet, and talking to a culturally responsive doctor, I feel less terrified and more open to keeping this baby and getting prepared for possible medical complications.

It occurred to me today even with a "perfect" baby, you never know what can happen in the future. With Muhammad, we didn't know we would have to get his allergies treated, but we found good resources, made a homemade formula, took him to over thirty NAET treatments with Dr. Levy and Dr. Askari, and he is doing great now. We had no preparation or prior knowledge of that, but we worked it out together. Tariq and I are great parents, and we can become even better parents with this child and any challenges we may face.

Tariq is leaning toward termination, but I am not comfortable with ending the life of this baby. If the baby did not make it, that's one thing, but to purposely abort it because of down syndrome and our own ignorance—I don't think I can live with myself and make that decision. I know we must do what is right for us, but I have to follow my instinct.

This baby is growing inside of me. Islamically the technicality may say there is no soul yet, but I see and feel this child with fingers, toes, arms, legs, a head, a brain, and a heart right now. Granted, the baby is still young, but I am its mother, and I feel protective. Tariq said he wants us to be on the same page. The page I am on has more information than his page about DS. DS people are whole people, and that extra chromosome can affect certain genes, but we won't know until it is older, but therapy can start as early as one to two months old to help with muscle tone, motor skills, etc.

I want Tariq to be open to information and not be so quick to abort our child. It begs the question, where is our faith? Don't we believe Allah knows best and would not give us a child we could not help nurture and love? I don't want to argue with my husband about a child we both agreed to have. It is our child, and yes, we have a responsibility to our family, but that baby can live and lead a normal life inshallah.

I spoke with a board member from GiGi's House, a nonprofit center for children with DS and their families. She has an eight-year-old son with DS. He has minor impacts from DS but talks normally, goes to school, and does well. She said it's not easy, but if they get early help, the impact of DS is less. Granted, her son did not have any heart conditions, which is a big concern for our baby. She offered to have us meet her at GiGi's House.

Yes, life might be simpler if we ended the pregnancy, but not easier. Either road has unknowns. Having lost baby Oliver, I feel like this is it for me as it relates to having children. Maybe God is testing our fortitude and faith in preparation for something down the road. I remember when baby Oliver died, and I thought my life was over. It took time, but I moved on, looked back, and saw the beauty in that experience and how it made me appreciate my Muhammad and children in general and all the advocacy work I did after that. Maybe this is my path. I must walk in my truth.

SEPTEMBER 2, 2013, MONDAY, LABOR DAY

Today I told my dad what was going on, and he burst into tears. I have never had an emotional moment with him. That was the first time I felt like I had a dad that cared for me as a father should. It was a moment. I hate it came through tragedy, but I learned my dad is sensitive. He told me he supports me no matter what we decide to do. That felt great to know.

Tariq and I watched a documentary on DS this morning on YouTube. Tariq wants us to decide on terminating or not before we get the amnio results. I understand we only have a week to get it done, and we will be right at day 120. That feels so wrong in my heart, yet I know, I guess, we could not handle the unknown outcome. I told Tariq I could not predict the outcome of how and who I will be after a termination. Right now, I want everything in my life to stop and just sit in quiet solitude. I don't want to rush back to work. I need time to rest, recuperate, and refocus. If we plan the termination for September 12 or 13, I will take two weeks off.

SEPTEMBER 5, 2013, THURSDAY, 11:23 P.M.
Today, I had the amnio done. When the needle entered my abdomen, it wasn't bad until the doctor pushed through my uterus. He pulled out about half a cup of fluid. You could see the baby swatting the needle on the monitor. Afterward, the cramping was so bad. On the way home, it got a little better. Tariq and I picked Muhammad up from daycare after going to Dairy Queen. Tariq handled everything for the evening while I slept until 9:00 p.m. I researched how to increase amnio fluid, so I am drinking a lot and will get some stevia tomorrow and drink tea with it.

SEPTEMBER 10, 2013, TUESDAY, 6:21 A.M.—AMNIOCENTESIS
We got the results of the amnio last night. It confirms trisomy 21. My baby has down syndrome. Tariq and I talked late into the evening. We kept checking in and rating ourselves on a scale of one to ten where we were leaning for termination, trying for another pregnancy, or keeping the baby. We saw

we were leaning toward termination with no more pregnancy tries. Our family unit will be three. There is so much to handle in this short period of time. I will tell my boss Janice after tomorrow I will need to be off work for minimally two weeks. That's all the vacation and sick leave I can spare, although a month would be better. *I am forever changed!*

SEPTEMBER 26, 2013, THURSDAY, 11:35 P.M.—HE HAS A RIGHT TO LIVE

During the last two weeks, Tariq and I have visited GiGi's Down Syndrome Playhouse to do more investigation of life with a Down Syndrome child. We saw so many sweet little children. Most were babylike, but they were two or three years old. The parents were eager to share with us. There was only one African American family there and probably fourteen White families. We also visited an Emory Genetic Counselor. They went through the ins and outs of what down syndrome is, the particulars about health concerns, and what we can do specifically for therapy, when to start therapy, and resources to help us financially. I also called multiple abortion clinics, and they explained the actual process. It was a violent procedure for the baby at fifteen weeks and just too much for me to consider doing once it was all laid out for me.

The Islamic 120-day mark passed on September 14th, when the soul has entered the baby. We learned and saw enough to know intellectually we thought we could end it, but knowing what that meant, no, we cannot. I cannot do that to this child, soul or no soul. We are moving forward with the pregnancy. We decided to share our journey. I told my immediate family about the diagnosis we received. I sent an email to some of the first managers at work sharing what we are going through.

I am still wondering if we are making the right choice. Are we going to be able to support this son? Yes, it is another boy. Are we being fair to Muhammad, having a child with a disability? Will the responsibility of a disabled little brother be too much for him and for us? I wonder if we had done the termination, would I be feeling the same confusion? It would be final. Allah knows best. Our son has just as much right to live as I, so although I could change my mind, what does that say about me? People and family would understand, but would I ever forgive myself for giving up on his life before he had a chance to live it? Sacrifice is what I am feeling.

We are not going to be able to raise this child alone. We will need the support of our families on both sides and friends, and not just for occasional babysitting. We will need everyone to really step up and support us with Muhammad and take him out and for weekends, come over and stay with the kids so Tariq and I can take the baby to therapy and maybe go on a date occasionally. And yes, we need to find a landscaping company, housekeeper, pest control service, and get these overdue home tasks done before the year is out.

CHAPTER 12

Higher Powered

OCTOBER 6, 2013, SUNDAY, 10:53 P.M.

I find myself searching for pictures of Black boys with DS. I am trying to imagine how my little guy will look. I also look at Muhammad and think, how similar and different will the DS impact how they will look like brothers? Muhammad is so handsome, I long for the DS not to be as apparent. I see a lot of kids have big mouths and glasses. I have seen some cute DS kids. I hope I am not being vain but just a protective mother wondering how her child will fair in a world that can be so mean to children with special needs.

Last night, I sent an email out to family and friends about the diagnosis of DS. It went out to 115 people. I was trying to cover important friends and people in our Islamic community. I have had positive responses. I want to educate people about DS. I also started an outline for a book about my joys and pains of motherhood, called *My Three Sons*. My goal is to write the book before the baby comes in February. I want to find a cowriter(s) such as a high-risk obstetrician, midwife, genetic counselor.

Here is the email:

Date: 10/05/2013 23:12 (GMT-06:00)
Subject: Tiffany Pregnancy Update

Greetings Family and Friends,

The road of life is filled with twists and turns. My life is no exception. Mine and Tariq's love is so strong, so we decided to have another child despite all the challenges I have faced having children and having already lost my first son. Presently, I am nineteen weeks pregnant with another son. Things have been going well generally, but on August 28, we received notification the results of a DNA blood test I took, because of my age, came back positive for T21 or Down Syndrome (DS).

We have gone through a myriad of emotions from disbelief to anguish, and with good information, we have moved to a place of understanding and resolve. We are continuing with our pregnancy and recognize we are good parents, and we will be even better parents as we raise a child with special needs. God never gives you more than you can handle, and we know we are truly blessed to begin this walk of faith.

Since the first news, we decided to have an amniocentesis to clearly verify the results. It confirmed the positive DS diagnosis. We have met with a genetic counselor, so we are informed of the "potential" for issues related to our son's health. Just this past Tuesday, we had a full anatomical ultrasound, and he was incredibly active and all his organs are developing fine so far.

Generally, the DS does not impact the pregnancy unless he shows some sort of development issue with his heart, which may require early delivery. Fifty percent of DS babies have a congenital heart defect. Everything is truly wait and see until he is born, including any cognitive and developmental delays. DS is a spectrum diagnosis. Our plan is to start speech, occupational, and physical therapies as early as one month old. As a family, we are also learning sign language to bridge the gap between his understanding language and wanting to communicate and his verbal language development, which may be delayed.

We have also started a blog to educate and inform family and friends about our journey as well as garner support in the form of prayers, positive comments we will use to help us through the tough times that may lie in the future, and some essential baby items we realized we would depend on much longer than with a typical baby.

There is no traditional shower planned (that I know of), but we will invite everyone to meet him after he is born.

I hope you will accept our apology for notifying you this way. I wish I could call and talk to every one of you, but everyone is busy with their own lives, and it takes time to adjust and know what to say. We are positive and hope you will take the news in stride like we have and continue to check in on us, call us, send your well wishes as every child is a trust with God, and we honor his trust in us with this child.

Walking in faith!

Tiffany and Tariq Abdullah

After Thanksgiving 2013, I started to reflect more about where I was the previous year at that time. I was pregnant and planning for my medical leave, then parental leave for our new son. We don't name our children until they are born, so he was just little man. Thanksgiving of 2013 was going to be in Detroit. We were going to drive up with Muhammad, Zacharia, and Amira.

I went for my then biweekly ultrasound, and the baby was still very small to be twenty-four weeks. They continued to watch him and me very closely and told me traveling was not a good idea with his small size. Our trip to Detroit was off, and we decided to cook a small dinner and stay home. Tariq's cousins were in town, so we invited them over for dinner.

Since October, I had been using a doppler for hearing the baby's heartbeat each evening when I got home from work. After about twenty-seven weeks, it started to get harder for me to find his heartbeat. This was concerning to me, but I did not tell Tariq just yet. He had been attending all the appointments with me except the last one. As my anxiety about losing the baby increased, I made sure he would be at the next ultrasound with me.

I was supposed to go on medical leave on December 20, 2013. My midwife wanted me on bed rest before then, but I would have used up all my FMLA and would not have had time at home with the baby. Given the baby had down syndrome, I had to expect the unexpected. Each year Georgia State University closes for winter break, so my last day of work would have been the nineteenth. On the seventeenth of December, we had the annual department holiday party. After the party, I had a scheduled ultrasound. Tariq was taking the train down to meet me so we would not have two cars. I was already nervous about the increasing difficulty of finding his heartbeat, so I needed Tariq there in case things escalated, which was what my intuition was telling me.

I went in for the ultrasound, and they took a long time getting measurements and checking blood vessels. I knew something was wrong. We were the last couple left in the office, and the doctor called us in to review the ultrasound. He was waiting on a call back from my midwife, Ms. Marsha, and she was on hold as we came into the office. The doc explained to her and us the baby was small and what they called growth restricted. Most likely because of the DS.

In addition, I have protein S deficiency, which adds more risk to the baby if my blood is not transferring enough oxygen to him. Throughout the pregnancy, I was giving myself heparin shots twice a day and taking baby aspirin to thin my blood. The doctor let us know he was in distress and his blood was staying in the heart and lungs, meaning he was not getting enough oxygen.

It was time for him to be delivered. I didn't need the doctor to tell me, but he did. Tariq and I were to go at once to Atlanta Medical Center for monitoring. This was about 5:00 p.m. We held hands and took a deep breath. Our relationship had been tested so far in having to make difficult decisions and weed through difficult emotions at every point in this pregnancy.

We left with admission papers, and our son would be borne by emergency C-section. It was my first C-section, and I was very nervous about such a traumatic surgery. On the way into the hospital, Tariq and I knew I would not be able to eat tomorrow, so we stopped at Whole Foods on Ponce and bought $50 worth of healthy food. I ate three times that night.

They kept me on a doppler to check the baby. They did a full ultrasound at 4:00 a.m., and by 8:00 a.m. Ms. Marsha, my midwife, was in the room. She told us the baby had to come out as soon as possible. They were waiting for Dr. Lorenza, who was her attending physician, to be available, which was about noon. At noon he came in to review the findings. We discovered we knew some of the same people because he went to Meharry in Nashville for medical school. We were the same age also. I told him frankly I wanted a small incision and not to "jack me up" because I had seen some awful C-section scars from friends. He assured me I would be bikini ready by spring.

At 1:00 p.m., I was on my way into the operating room. Tariq was there and snuck into the operating room early. I was glad at his persistence because I was shaking from my nervousness. Dr. Lorenza made me comfortable, and I was made extremely comfortable by the fine-ass anesthesia resident. I mean, Allah had me in good hands with three Black kings— my fine husband, nice doctor, and model-like anesthesia doctor. I felt fine in surgery. I did not feel a thing. Tariq, needing to always be in the mix, stood up and watched every gory bit of it. He even got splashed with blood across his face. About 1:30 p.m., we heard the small but powerful cry of our son born into this world. He was only one pound and 14 ounces.

He was breathing on his own with a little difficulty. They brought him over to me, and I kissed his little face. He looked like me but just tiny. Tariq stayed with him as they finished up my surgery. They took him to the NICU (neonatal intensive care unit) and me to recovery.

There was some type of power surge in me after he was born. I was determined to keep the promises I made for him, to Allah, and to my son Muhammad. He was born on December 18, meaning my two living sons' birthdays were only two days apart. I had planned a three-year-old birthday party for Muhammad at Chuck E. Cheese for December 21. The baby hadn't been due until February, so I had no reason not to plan a party for Muhammad. I knew I had to be out of the hospital by Friday afternoon to make it to Muhammad's party. It was Wednesday when I delivered the baby. Even through the pain, I was determined to stand up and walk.

I fought through the pain and was released, with some prodding of the nurse, that Friday morning. I made sure I was her first discharge. I made it to Muhammad's birthday party, but I was fully medicated to do it. I had the entire family there to support us, but I wanted Muhammad to have a great birthday, and he did.

ATTENDING TO NAS-SEERU

After I got out of the hospital, I had to be driven to see the baby because you cannot drive until about three weeks after a C-section. The first time I went into the NICU was one of the scariest and most intimidating moments of my life. You feel so helpless as a mother to see your tiny baby with all these devices attached to them and have to ask to do anything for your child. It was almost too much to bear.

One night Tariq and I went to the hospital around 10:00 p.m. because they fed him at 11:00 p.m. I was pumping as much as I could and was getting a small amount but more than with Muhammad. I was taking herbs and eating a lactogenic diet to help increase my milk. I had a breast reduction in December of 2004, so it was nine years later that I was trying to breastfeed for my third pregnancy. I was getting about two oz every session, which was enough for a preemie. The nurse on duty that night was very talkative and opinionated. I had just had an emergency C-section, and this was about five days after I had the baby, and I had not held him yet.

The nurse started to talk to me about pumping on a schedule, which is what I was doing, and he needed more milk. She even questioned us about why we had come so late and told us we missed him with his eyes open when he was awake. It was so much, and she was so loud and extra. She set me off, and I began to cry. I even wanted to leave, but Tariq stepped in, and when I went into the pumping room he talked to her sternly, to say the least.

She apologized when I came out, and she let me hold my baby for the first time. He was so small and delicate with the feeding tubes attached to him.

He was breathing on his own for nineteen days until it was discovered he was refluxing into his lungs. He was off and on CPAP to help support his breathing. Earlier in the pregnancy, we discovered his heart was formed normally. We were in good shape other than him growing and getting fed through a tube until his reflux stopped or surgically was corrected. We found out he had pulmonary hypertension. Pulmonary hypertension (PH) is high blood pressure in the arteries of the lungs that can lead to right heart failure.

I sat day after day with my baby named Nas-Seeru by Tariq. I stayed by his side in the NICU, learning to care for him as much as I could. Changing diapers, doing skin-to-skin contact, and pumping and pumping to give him breast milk, which was the best for him. He grew very well, and by his original due date in February he was eight pounds.

He had many ups and downs with the occasional infections, a couple of blood transfusions, but in early February he was doing better. I was able to give him a bath, and he was wearing clothes for the first time. He was in an open bed from the incubator he had been in for two months. He knew his mommy, and he was vocal and cried when the nurses would mess with him to do the number of procedures, X-rays, echocardiograms, blood tests, etc., to keep him alive. It was truly amazing what medicine can do for these babies.

Tariq had to work and take care of Muhammad. He was there some evenings with Nas, and the family visited occasionally, but I battled that NICU routine alone most days. Every time I walked into the NICU and saw the nurses around his bed, I felt I would faint because I didn't know what I would have to face that day. The stress was unbearable. I started to get very ill off and on. There were three times I was so sick I could not go to the hospital for at least a week each time because I had a fever and was not allowed in.

Nas got sicker and had to go on a ventilator. I was so stressed, there was no way to express it. Tariq was trying to care for me at home, but the fevers were getting higher, and I was getting weaker. During the worst episode, as I call it, I thought I was going to die. Tariq took me to the doctor, and we decided I needed to go into the hospital for evaluation. The pain in my head was so intense with the fevers and fatigue. I was overcome with worry. Throughout all of this, I was praying, talking to Allah… begging Allah to save my baby. I was so worried I ended up in the hospital myself on February 14, 2014.

I could see Atlanta Medical Center, where Nas was from my window at Emory in Midtown. I was going in and out of the most painful migraines I had ever had. I talked to Allah, asking Him to heal me and find out what was wrong. I continued to pray. My soul knew Nas had his own path. I was just a vehicle. I had to let go and allow Allah to make the decisions that needed to be made. I was not in control, and all my worrying was only making me ill. I finally received a diagnosis.

MY SECOND ANGEL

I got a little better, enough to get out of the hospital and get back to the NICU to get back to Nas. He was very sick and now had to be intubated with the ventilator, meaning he needed a tube down his throat to his lungs to breathe. He started to need more and more percent of oxygen to keep his pulse ox up. On March 3, we moved him to Children's Hospital at Scottish Rite so he could receive the best care. The pulmonary hypertension was severe. Tariq and I essentially moved into the sleeping quarters of the hospitals around April 10.

On April 12, Tariq's birthday, we went out for dinner and had a serious talk about Nas's prognosis and preparing ourselves for the worst. Tariq and I sat by his side taking turns reading the Qur'an. Tariq told me to go get some rest, but he came to get me about 1:00 a.m. on April 13. Nas was not doing well. I came into the NICU and asked them to turn off all the pumps, remove all the sensors, and let me hold my son. The nurses quietly and quickly did as requested. I had not held him since I bathed him in February.

They handed him to me. He was big now. He was so beautiful, and he looked just like Muhammad. I held him so close to my heart. I kissed his face, his arms, and his hands. All the team left us and removed all the medical devices from our area. It was just the three of us. I held him, and Tariq continued reciting the Qur'an. The only monitor attached was his heart monitor. After fifteen minutes, his heart failed.

My sweet baby fought for four months but was now our angel. Suphanallah, I was so thankful to be there by his side. We gave him full Islamic funeral rites of ghusl (bathed) and kafin (shrouding) before his body was cool. That was something we had not planned to do, but he passed in the middle of the night, and we did it together.

The hospital staff was so supportive. They gave us everything we needed. I kept a little bottle of frankincense and myrrh in my purse we used to perfume him. We completed the rites and carried him ourselves down to the morgue. The Islamic funeral home picked him up later in the morning. Tariq and I went back to the sleeping room and cried our eyes out. No one can prepare you for losing a child, and for me, a second child.

We left the hospital and got home about 5:30 a.m. We showered, cried some more, and made fajah prayer. I prayed behind Tariq in our prayer/living room, and when I stood up, I saw a vision of Tariq and two young men standing alongside him. One had jet black wavy hair, and one had light sandy brown hair. Both had on long white thobes, or long Islamic shirts men wear. I smiled through my tears.

Shukran Allah (Thank you, God) for showing me my sons, Oliver and Nas-Seeru, were together and all right. Muslims believe everyone who passes, no matter their age, will become thirty-three, and this is the age those young men looked to be. It was a moment that soothed my soul. I was able to sleep after fajr prayer, and when I woke up, we started planning. We did what was prescribed and buried Nas within seventy-two hours. Our family and friends surrounded the kids and us with love and support.

Nas's death, unlike the death of my first son, made my faith stronger. From the age of seven, when I had that out-of-body experience, I learned there was more to life than what we see. It was what I experienced. Life is great, but Allah is greater. Oh, there were so many mercies that Allah gave us. Every moment I had with Nas. All the prayers from thousands of people who were praying for him and me and our family. We had time to prepare as best we could for his passing. I know we made the right decision to let him live out the life Allah had for him.

I have the hardest time when I focus on the pain in my physical body. After his passing, so many shared with me the hadith about babies who die, telling me he is under the care of Prophet Ibrahim and one day I will be reunited with my sons and the other baby I miscarried. Oh, Allah has given me peace with that knowledge.

I still cry, and I still get sad, but less than the day before. I want to continue to grow stronger in my deen. My life continues to be a living story. Nas passing was a new beginning. I was always a Muslim with a little "m," but losing my son made me a MUSLIM with all CAPS. On the day of Resurrection, some hadiths say I will be reunited, and my sons will intercede for me until Allah grants me entrance into paradise. Oh, I think of them and smile, because Allah is the best of planners. I asked Allah to continue to make my Islamic faith stronger and more focused. The soul is stronger than the body, and when we focus on preparing our souls, there is incomprehensible strength one receives.

The last four months have been the hardest of my life. My baby, Nas-Seeru, passed away last Sunday with Tariq and me by his side. He was such a strong boy. He fought hard, but Allah knows best. I was unsure if we could give him a good life, and he was on the ventilator for so long I was afraid he had brain damage. I will forever love him. And I long for the day I see him and my son Oliver in Paradise.

I am surprised at how well I am doing, but I do have a sense of relief knowing he is safe, happy, healthy, and waiting on me. I am more committed to being a great mother for Muhammad. I have been gone and distant the past four months caring for Nas. Muhammad deserves my full attention now. He also lost his little brother. He had nightmares the night after the funeral. All the grandparents were here to support him, Vernest and Shirley, my parents, and Hussein and Anisa, Tariq's parents. My mother took her shahada with me as witness because she was so overcome with the beauty of the Islamic funeral. She wants to be buried as a Muslim. Takbir-Allah Akbar. I am proud of her.

Mine and Tariq's relationship strengthened through this trial. We celebrated our fifth anniversary yesterday. Last Saturday was his thirty-sixth birthday. Birthday, death, anniversary—the cycle of life all in one week. My faith and eagerness to enhance my deen are inspired by Nas. I owe it to him to live my best life and be the best person Allah has created me to be. There is a question of whether we have another child. Tariq said no more children. Only Allah knows best.

I am thirty-eight. I have lost two of three children, including an ectopic pregnancy that required surgery. Maybe I am meant to birth angels. Maybe it has something to do with the out-of-body experience I had when I was seven years old. I have always had a spiritual connection to God and a knowing there was more to this world since that experience as a child. I try not to frame it as: Why does God keep taking my children? That question is negative. But knowing they are waiting on me gives me peace.

Maybe they were sick, too sick to live in this world. Or maybe this world was too sick for them. I am trying to find out more about my health. I pray answers will be revealed. I will write a memoir on my experience one day, inshallah.

Tariq's mother, Mariam-Anisa/Janice Petross passed away unexpectedly on November 9, 2014. May Allah give her the highest seat in paradise. I am so grateful to have spent that time with her. She was a brilliant woman and did so much good work for her community. She raised a beautiful family, and I honor her and miss her laugh.

BACK AT WORK

A few weeks before Nas passed, Tariq and I began seeing a marriage counselor for lots of reasons. We stopped the sessions when I got sick, so our next session was after Nas passed. When we told the doctor about the baby passing away, it was challenging for him to get through the session. In that session, we discussed whether I should go back to work. I thought it was better to have more time off, but Tariq thought it was best I had something to keep me occupied. I was in a vulnerable state of being and did not have any fight left in me, so I went along with his suggestion, which seemed reasonable at the time.

I went back to work on May 5, 2014, three weeks after Nas passed. It had been four and a half months since I had worked. I moved into a new cube with a terrific view of downtown Atlanta. I poured myself into my work for the rest of the year. It paid off. I completed a huge project for the chief innovation officer, Phil Ventimiglia. My boss's boss, Julian Allen, was creating a new center, the Center for Excellence in Teaching and Learning (CETL). He had a position open, and Janice, my boss, encouraged me to apply for it. I spoke with Julian about the role.

He said, "I think you would be fine in the role, Tiffany, but tell me what you really want to do."

"You mean, create a job for myself in CETL?" I replied.

He responded, "Sure, give me an idea of what you think you can bring to CETL. Do you think a week is enough time to show me something?"

"Yes, I can definitely put something together," I said enthusiastically. I spent the next week researching jobs and teams. I called mentors. I ultimately crafted a team I called *Learning Community Development*. I got promoted to manager of Learning Community Development. One of my first projects was coordinating the opening week celebration for CETL in April 2015. The opening week was a hit.

I was doing my best to juggle everything. I was trying to be a good mother to Muhammad, who was now four. Zach and Amira were coming home every other weekend because they were school age now. Tariq was growing Tarchitects and working well out of the home office. I was pushing down all my grief into my work. That was starting to show signs of failure.

I was agitated at home and depressed. I was spending a lot of time daydreaming about Nas and seeing him in our day-to-day life just to cope. I dreamed about Muhammad showing him how to walk and tie his shoes. I would not allow Tariq to donate the baby items. I was still holding on to a baby who had died. Mentally, I was coming unglued, but I was masking that at work.

We had slowed in our counseling once I started working but started going more often as my mood became contentious and more argumentative at home. The depression, mood, and overworking myself were taking a toll on my health. I started getting sick again in the spring of 2015 and had to take a leave of absence from work to get myself together.

I went on leave for seven weeks in the summer of 2015. I did an intensive deep dive of counseling over the seven weeks as well as lots of doctor's appointments to make sure my health was under control. I slept for a week straight and just sat in my grief for my baby Nas and baby Oliver. I cried until there wasn't a tear left in my body. I had to let go of the grief for those babies and for the perfect family I longed for and focus on the beautiful family right in front of me.

Part of my recovery was focusing again on my faith. I began taking Islamic courses before Ramadan that summer. Focusing on my taqwa—"being conscious and cognizant of God"—helped me keep the depression at bay as well as making my salaat "Islamic prayers." I also began reading the Qur'an more regularly and listening to gospel music again. I grew up singing in choirs when I was Christian, and just playing the music throughout the house and singing soothed my soul.

I went back to work and continued to excel. I got more promotions and won grants and awards. In 2017, I developed the Digital Learners to Leaders program, which is still going on as a course. The program has positively affected the lives of hundreds of students at Georgia State University. Tariq and I continued developing The Community Academy for Architecture and Design. We held a gala at Kennesaw State University in February 2018. It became an approved charter school in June 2018. We were honored by the Atlanta masjid for our work in the community.

It is amazing to look back and see how far we have come. God is Good.

CHAPTER 13

Conclusion

____

FORTITUDE

I was hopeful 2020 would be my level-up year. It would be my time to do the things I had been putting off as I worked multiple roles as a mother, wife, full-time professional, and entrepreneur. I resigned from my full-time position at Georgia State University in January 2020 after a very successful eight-year career to join my husband in our architecture firm as the chief operations officer. I ended my time there by being awarded the 2020 Carl Patton Presidential Award for Social Justice and Community Service for Outstanding Staff at Georgia State University. It felt incredible to leave on top. I stayed on as a consultant to help my former team transition to a virtual model of the Digital Learners to Leaders program.

My mother had her sixty-seventh birthday in early January, and I had our oldest family photos restored for her present. I turned forty-four in late January 2020 and celebrated by bringing my Momma into Atlanta from Nashville and having a fancy dinner at Nan Thai, a restaurant in downtown

Atlanta. I also celebrated with my January birthday sister-friends by seeing Oprah Winfrey's Life in Focus Tour at the State Farm Arena with 50,000 people. It was an awesome and inspiring day and a great beginning to 2020. Now, gathering in large numbers comes with a higher risk level and new safety protocols. Our way of life has been changed.

On February 29, 2020, I took my then nine-year-old son Muhammad to the movies, one of our favorite mommy and son dates. We saw *The Call of the Wild* and *Bad Boys 3* as a bonus. We sat for a few minutes after the movie ended. I needed to gather my thoughts about a virus circulating through the news. I gently let my nine-year-old know this would be our last time going to the movies for an unknown period. He asked if it had to do with the virus, and I said yes.

Tariq was in Detroit and was returning on an 11:00 p.m. flight. He had been there for two weeks working in the new office for our architecture firm. We opened our second office there in late 2019. I was flying out the next morning to Seattle, where the virus supposedly entered the country. I was always thinking about what we would need in cases of emergency. This was a different and uncharted road for our family.

Through the second movie, I researched how to make masks—since there were none in stock anywhere—and prep for a pandemic, a new word in our lexicon. I was making a list. Muhammad and I left the movies and drove two miles to Sam's Club, where I bought over $300 of cleaning supplies in preparation for what was coming. Everyone in the store was staring at my flat cart filled with disinfectants, bleach, rubber gloves, alcohol, hand soap, essential food, bottled water, and, of course, toilet tissue. Within a few weeks, most of those cleaning items were out of stock.

The next day, March 1, I was to start a three-leg speaking tour to Seattle, New York City, and Austin, Texas, during the first two weeks of March. While literally taxiing on the runway en route to Seattle, the first conference was canceled. I had no choice at that point. I was going to Seattle. I decided to stay overnight since the hotel was essentially empty, and I was not about to turn right back around for another five-hour flight. I connected with my friend, Kamani, who I had not seen in ten years. We met at her condo near Pike's Place Market and walked to a Thai restaurant. The dinner was incredible, and we had a lovely night catching up.

Jet lag kicked in about 11:00 p.m. Pacific time, and it was still a forty-five-minute drive back to my hotel. We said our good-byes, hugged, and promised to keep in touch. I left the next morning for Atlanta. After my twenty-four-hour cross-country trip, I made it home, and my husband and I decided I would not be taking any of the other trips. By the end of that week, all the trips and conferences were canceled anyway.

The country began to spiral after that. The schools shut down in mid-March, and parents were on their own. Most school districts, particularly those in Georgia, were ill-prepared for online learning. As the cofounders of a soon-to-be charter school, we were able to educate our son from home.

We paused on our school, The Community Academy for Architecture and Design (TCAAD), to see how things would fair for schools. In March, we were about to hire the school's principal and finalize a nearly million-dollar loan to renovate the school facility on Memorial Drive, only eight minutes from our home. I was particularly worried about having this large loan and a possible empty school building if children were online. The margins are already slim for running a charter school.

At the time, we didn't know there would be large amounts of federal funds to help schools. We were a small governing board who needed to make decisions then. I had just left my job at Georgia State University. Now the family was fully dependent on our family business at the beginning of a pandemic. We had to focus all our efforts on one thing, Tarchitects, which would be our only income. We were never going to make money from the school. The school was philanthropic. We had an idea to do a virtual model. We thought we would be able to resubmit an amended petition to the State of Georgia Charter School Commission in the spring of 2021.

In May, the video surfaced of the murder of George Floyd at the hands of Minneapolis Police Officers led by Derek Chauvin. Minneapolis was my home for seven years before I moved to Atlanta, so I was particularly disturbed by Mr. Floyd's brutal murder on camera and the subsequent protests, riots, and burning of communities in Minneapolis and throughout the country and world. George Floyd calling for his mother under distress was a rallying call to me, and to mothers I know, and some of us began meeting in July of 2020 and started a leadership network of Black Muslim women called Era of Woman. We started studying together and figuring out a way to help our community heal and be restored. In October 2021, we launched our first event, A Mother's Prayer Rally, in Atlanta while planning for other rallies across the nation in major cities. Inshallah "God Willing," our network of motherhood leadership will continue to grow and show results that help to restore, advance, prepare, and protect the African American community.

By late July, COVID-19 was running rampant, and people were dying in large numbers. I was suffering from post-traumatic stress disorder from increased violence and the COVID-19 deaths. We finally heard back from the state of Georgia about TCAAD, and they wanted us to resubmit in two weeks, and given everyone's stress level, it was not plausible. As a family, we had to focus on our health, mental and physical, as well as our board members. We decided to voluntarily relinquish our charter with the state of Georgia and focus on our primary business, our architecture firm.

When we made the decision, it felt like a thousand ton of bricks were taken off our shoulders. We worked for ten years developing the model. Since the summer of 2020, we have piloted the virtual model but as a private school. It has been successful. We are partnering with some national programs and local museums to bring our expertise for culturally responsive architectural exposure to a broader base of students. We understand TCAAD is a long-term endeavor, and we pray for a strong board and for our children to continue that legacy as we work on teaching and showing them how to build a strong community.

For the rest of 2020, we were running our business and home-schooling Muhammad and spending quality time boating to get us out of the house. I was researching for the book and had to push back on the publishing date. My social circle was closing in as travel became more difficult and riskier. I became a homebody and didn't go out unless it was to get something for the house or for a special occasion. The isolation started to take a toll on me because I am naturally very social and much more sensitive than most people would know. It's for those reasons I turned inward, and I began writing more and became even more reflective. It was the best use of my time. I didn't want to come out of this pandemic with nothing to show for it except extra pounds and a neat home. I wanted to complete something for me. I hope this book will also lay the foundation for renewing our heritage related to the bean pie and laying the foundation for that business.

I presold my bean pies in small batches, which sold out daily.

It was in 2021 I renewed my intention to complete this book. I found new information from Ancestry.com and compiled a family tree with over 365 people on both my family's maternal and paternal sides. This book only touches on the maternal side. Even as I go to print, there is a group of people helping me with research in Opelika, Alabama. As more research is discovered, I may publish a second edition or add more information about the family through my website, TheBean-Pie.com or TiffanyGreenAbdullah.com. This research into my family is a life-long journey, and there are so many more stories to uncover and tell.

The Ancestry DNA tests revealed who my true biological grandfather is. I had a conversation with that family, and I hope to continue that dialogue. I do not want anything from them except to know them now. I don't hold any hostility about what may have happened between him and my grandmother. I just want to know who my connections are and if there are health issues we should be aware of. I believe it is important to know for my son and me as we age.

The process of writing this book has been cathartic and downright hard. I am grateful for my journals and the depth of details I could recount for this book. Some days and some weeks, I could not write because the topics were challenging to think about and relive. Writing about my babies in such depth was like living it all over again. I cried so many times when I finished certain passages and even just by rereading it. Writing about my grandma was challenging because it had been nearly thirty years since I thought so extensively about her. I used the concept of astral projection to detach my mind from my physical body and to send it to distant places or into alternate realities to write about the places and scenes I wrote about. There would be days this would have me emotionally exhausted, and it would take a day to recover to write again.

FAMILY

This has been a lonely endeavor. I look forward to the reader joining me in this world. I wrote this book for my family and healing—not for acclaim.

I pray in the future, as my children get older and have their own children, they read this book humbly without judgment because, just as I have shown, we all will face challenges and obstacles, some seen and some unseen.

Please do not judge those who came before you. We had our tests, and you will have yours. I want you to know family, faith, fortitude, and forgiveness will help you get through your tests also. Write your stories so the next generation will know you and remember you. Please continue this as our legacy.

We opened with Aunt Daisy. It was her bean pies that inspired all of this. The bean pie is more than a pie. The bean pie is eating history and culture. Her story and the bean pie have been hidden from history, and I hope she is proud of me for stepping out and telling it. I want her to know the sacrifices she made have not been in vain. I want her to know everything she did for my grandma and for my momma got me to this place in my life. It is a full circle.

Grandma Shirley was a beautiful young woman who got mixed up with an older man who apparently fathered two children with her, and she was married off to Wilbur Green to keep up appearances. She divorced Wilbur and married my granddaddy, Jesse Boyd. They had a complicated relationship in the early days, but by the time I came along she was older and somewhat wiser yet still struggling with drug addiction. She was a good mother and a good grandmother. She took care of her family no matter what was going on with her. Granddaddy was always around and supporting the family when needed. I cherish the memory of him attending my undergraduate graduation from Vanderbilt University in 1998.

My Momma Shirley is a strong woman who endured so much to raise my brother and me. I love and appreciate her openness through the process of this book. I would annoy her with tons of calls pushing her to remember details she had not thought about in decades. She is a fighter and continues to fight to get stronger from the most recent health challenges she has faced. We all faced them with her.

My story is not very different from my elders. I had more formal education and more opportunities, but I am learning more about myself through their stories. The common threads of family, faith, and fortitude bind us through the generations.

FORGIVENESS

Forgiveness is the thread I offer to the link. Forgiveness is what I have learned is needed for healing the trauma so many of us have experienced as children through adulthood. It is a way of going back in time and rewriting the wrongs done to us and by us. Forgiveness is not time travel. It is not a perfect method. It's certainly not a do-over, but it's a step toward a better tomorrow. Forgiveness can help this generation acknowledge for ourselves and for our ancestors, "We been through some shit," either at the hands of others or at our own hands. Healing our ACEs, or Adverse Childhood Experiences, take time, take patience, and take a reconnecting with one's own body to heal from trauma. I am not recommending any form of healing beyond working with a licensed therapist first. I have invested time and resources in years of therapy at different times in my life and for different reasons.

One of the advantages of this pandemic has been the wider availability of virtual therapy. I have gone through difficult periods without a therapist when I may have needed one but could not afford one. There are different techniques to help with forgiveness, including talking one on one with a person you have experienced trauma with or from, healing circles with a group of people, and talk therapy with a licensed therapist. If you need healing, do your own research to find the best solution that works for you culturally and financially. Finding an African American licensed therapist who takes insurance is very challenging, but sometimes the money must be secondary to taking care of yourself.

I hope I have not offended anyone with my honesty. I write from a place of healing and truth. My journals were the only place where I could be truly honest in my life. I am taking a risk opening myself to the world, but I do it knowing not everyone will like it, and that's okay. I hope it opens a space for dialogue.

FAITH

My life would be empty without faith. My faith has grown from my days as a child having that out-of-body experience, to bible study, to being baptized and growing into a Christian. I considered Islam as a teenager, but I was alone in my walk, and it was not the time for me to become a Muslim. It was not until I was thirty-three that I became a Muslim, one who submits to the will of Allah. I became a Muslim for myself, and it was the best decision for me then and now. There are so many misconceptions about what it is to be a woman in Islam. I have found out for myself that Allah wants to make everything easy for you. There are different ways to live as a Muslim, just as a Christian, a Jew, or any other spiritual path. I have found my balance over time, and I am still growing. I offer some foundational teachings of faith or Iman that are key to my understanding and growth.

"Iman" is the word "faith" from the Arabic language. It means to believe, to repose faith, to affirm His truth, to recognize, to rely on, or to submit to His commands. A Muslim has got to believe some fundamental issues. These are conclusively established by the Qur'anic and traditional evidence. One cannot become a Muslim without this set of beliefs.

Almighty Allah, the Greatest, says: "O you, who believe, have faith in Allah and His Messenger (PBUH—peace be upon him) and the book that He revealed to His messenger and the scripture which He revealed before. Whoever disbelieves in Allah, His angels, His books, His Messengers, and the last day has certainly gone far astray (Surah an-Nisa: ayat 136).

"It is understood Iman is affirmation and not merely belief. Affirmation includes the words of the heart, which is belief, and the actions of the heart, which is compliance" (Majmu' Al-Fatawa 7/638).

Belief in Allah: Muslims believe in one, unique, incomparable Allah, Who has no son or partner and that none has the right to be worshipped but Him alone. He is the true God, and every other deity is false. He has the most magnificent names and sublime perfect attributes. No one shares His divinity or His attributes. In the Qur'an, Allah describes himself: "Say, 'He is Allah, the One. Allah, to whom the creatures turn for their needs. He begets not, nor was He begotten, and there is none like Him" (Surah al-Ikhlas: Ayat 1–4).

Belief in fate or destiny: Muslims believe in fate, which is divine predestination, but this belief in divine predestination does not mean that human beings do not have free will. Rather, Muslims believe Allah has given human beings free will. This means they can choose right or wrong, and they handle their choices.

I have faith this book will do good for someone. It has done good for me to move on from so much shame and trauma. At forty-five at the time of writing, I am a woman empowered by my trauma and ready to help other people, especially other women, use their pain as power. It is time for healing and reclaiming our dignity. I am from a strong line of women. Otherwise, I would not be here. I am from the Balanta people in Guinea Bissau, the Mende and Temne people in Sierra Leone, the Mandinka people in Senegal. I am from the Scaife family in Alabama. I am from the Cantrell and Shark family in Arkansas. I am from the Ross family as well. We are not distant. We are only as far as our stories and as our knowledge. I looked back to regain their stories so that my sight could look further into the future. My connection to the past was lost, preventing my soul from seeing the future. My connection is now reattached and reaffirmed, and I have faith in the bright future ahead.

My prayer for the reader:

I pray whoever reads this book is blessed with an abundance of love and prosperity for their family.

I pray you receive healing from any trauma, and you turn your pain into power.

I pray you write your family's story and document your history for future generations.

I pray you gain in your faith, build up your family, grow in your fortitude, and let go of your pain so there is room for forgiveness.

I pray our family will have a holistic understanding of who we are and begin to heal.

Thank you for reading.

The Bean Pie: A Remembering of Our Family's Faith, Fortitude, and Forgiveness

PHOTOS (CHAPTER 8–13)

THESE PHOTOS ARE TO ENHANCE
THE STORY AND BE A HISTORICAL
RECORD OF THESE TIMES.

I enjoyed being back with my Aunties in Atlanta. They are a
lively bunch of ladies, Summer 2008.

I took this photo of
Tariq the night we
met when we were at
the coffee shop.

Meeting Tariq's children for the first
time. Amira is two and Zacharia is
nine months, March 2009.

Tariq and I spent his birthday in April 2009 at Panola State Park.

Mine and Tariq's first Eid together, September 2009.

Tariq traveled with me to Minneapolis for a business trip. My friends threw us a dinner (left to right—Jennifer White, Robert Lilligren, Tariq and me, Chanda, and Roland Baker, Demetrius Lewis, unknown person, Randy, and Kristina Fielding and Nimco Ahmed.) I miss my Minneapolis family.

Amira tired
from all the
house-hunting.

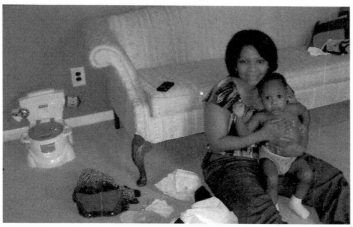

The early days in our new home, potty training, and teaching
Zach to walk.

Summer 2010 with
my sisters-in-law,
Sakinah and Nura,
nieces, and the
children at Belle
Isle in Detroit. I
was pregnant
with Muhammad.

Visiting Tariq's father, "Abu" Hussein, in Detroit.

Muhammad
looked like a
beach ball inside
of me. All my
besties at the
baby shower they
planned for me,
October 2010.

Momma with her Muhammad,
one hour after he was born,
December 2010.

Tariq and newborn
Muhammad. We were still at
the hospital.

Tariq, a new dad again with Muhammad shortly after we came home.

Tariq's mother, Anisa "Umm," stayed with us in Atlanta in 2011. We miss her dearly.

My baby Muhammad at three weeks old.

Tariq and Muhammad, age one.

My birthday sister Michelle and me. We worked as ushers when we were fifteen or sixteen.

Going to the Atlanta masjid fashion show, 2011.

My dad, a.k.a. "Paw-Paw," with Muhammad, 2012.

Michelle and Chad's crazy big wedding party, 2012.

My aunties and Momma are special ladies.
We have so much fun together, 2013.

Eid 2013.
Early in my
pregnancy
with Nas-
Seeru, 2013.

Muhammad breaks
his foot at age three.
The kids made the
day more enjoyable
for him going to
three different
doctors, 2013.

Abdullah family 2013.

Muhammad's third birthday party. I had a C-section with Nas three days before this party. The things a mother does for her children. It was special to have all the family and friends there, especially my mom and dad.

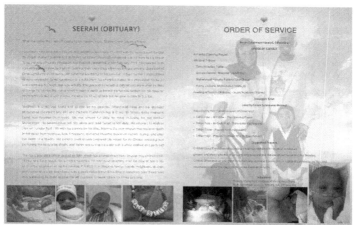

He lived a short life, but Nas strengthened our faith and marriage.

Mom, Dad, and I for Thanksgiving 2016.

TCAAD Benefit at
KSU, February 2018.

Of course Aunties DeDe and Melody
were there to support us.

Tariq and I received a
community service award
from the Atlanta Masjid
in 2018.

Momma came to Atlanta
to go to the grandparent's
luncheon at Muhammad's
school, 2019.

The best birthday dinner ever for my forty-fourth! This was the
last time Momma could come to Atlanta, January 2020.

The January birthday club sees Oprah (Aseelah and Raqayyah). Oprah and I share the same birthday, January 29.

Zach's thirteenth birthday was spent nearly killing myself at a rope course park in Nashville with my brother and nieces.

We spent Eid 2021 in Virginia with Tariq's brother Mansur, wife Jenn Layla, and sons Zayd and Amir.

Eid 2021 in Virginia. We spent the day with Abu and his family.

Our little family is so blessed, and even with our challenges, our children are growing into incredible young people, 2020.

I love this man more than I can ever express in words. Thank you, babe, for all you do for me, the family, and the community. I look forward to the decades to come!

Acknowledgments

My life has been blessed with many angels along the journey.

I want to give honor and praise to my ancestors. I have called out their names and asked for their aid and guidance on this journey to lead me in the right direction and give me the courage to tell these stories of family, faith, fortitude, and forgiveness.

A huge thank you to my husband, Tariq, who built me a room of my own, allowing me a space of light and love to dream and create in. Thank you to my "sun" Muhammad for being the sweetest and smartest little guy and a tech genius who helped me edit the images within this book.

Thank you to all my family who, over the years, have pulled money together to help me when I needed it and supported me through four cities. Special shout out to all my Aunties Deborah, Valerie, Delovely, Melody and Robbin, my brother Bernard and all my nieces as well as all my cousins.

Second, my girls, my sisters from other mothers... Anisha, Michelle, Vikki, Nikki, and Nia. You all have picked me up off the floor when life was hard, and you scream when there is something to celebrate. You all are my truth circle, and I love you all.

Thank you to Link Unlimited for giving kids like me a chance. Without the education you helped provide me, I am not sure I would have made it out of Chicago. Thank you for the friendships I hold most dear, many of which are Link Alum. Special shout out to Dr. Julie Welborn, and Roseanne and John Swain.

My time in Nashville was made easier by my cousin Darryl "Fujji" Griffin, who looked after me and let me live with him. You always have my back, and I thank you for everything seen and unseen you have done for me over the years.

There are so many people in Minneapolis that made an impact on my life and helped guide my direction, including Lea Hargett, Andrea Jenkins, Connie Kiser, Chanda Smith-Baker, Jennifer White, Robert Lilligren, VJ Smith, Randy Fielding, and Dr. John Taborn.

Atlanta is my home now. Thank you to the Atlanta Masjid community for accepting me and supporting the community work of Tariq and I. I appreciate the friendships I am developing here and the families our children are growing up with. Special shout out to Aseelah, Shaheerah, Zakiyyah, Carmen, Latonya, and so many more strong intelligent fly women in this community.

Thank you to my Georgia State University family, Janice Maxwell, Dr. Julian Allen, Phil Ventimiglia, Jackie Slaton, Keyonna Sutton, Kelly Robinson, Dr. Valora Richardson, Dr. Joyce King, Dr. Gholdie Muhammad, Dr. Brian Williams, Dr. Dana Salter, James Amaan, James Deegan, and all the students of PantherHackers and Digital Learners to Leaders. Thank you for supporting all my wild ideas and providing a place to fail fast and be innovative.

Thank you to my beta readers: Anita Rapier, Hillary McGuire, Quran Shakir, Vikki Stokes, Darryl Griffin, and Sarah Shay. Your feedback was vital to making this book better.

Thank you to New Degree Press for creating a book writing program. You all made the process achievable and supportive. Thank you for publishing this book.

Thank you to all the friends and family who encouraged me not to give up on this book.

And last, thank you to the one hundred people who believed in me enough to preorder this book. You made me not give up!

Shaheerah Williams	Dana Downing
Fatima Khokhar	Robert Turner Griffin Jr.
Khamishah Griffin	Aseelah Rashid
Makesha Dockery	Janice Maxwell
Michael Ruiz	Sabria Mills
Cliff Deese	Emily Muench
Robert Sheffield	Daisy Jack

Sherra Carey

Kim Foney

Sarah Shay

Maria Pullos

Stephanie Evans

Hillary McGuire Easom

Tariq Abdullah

Waigi Collins

Justin Lonsbury

Carla Griffin-Dean

Crystal 'Nyimah' Byrd

Anita Rapier

Sharron Downs

Darryl Griffin

Rasheedah Luqman

Raymond Lewis

Deborah Nunley

Brennen Dicker

Perla Tirado

Shelly-Ann Williams

Ronnie Reddish Jr.

Kenya King

Sumayyah Hill

Jennifer Black

Heidi Adelsman

Constance Jones

Frieda Muwakkil

Zarinah Nadir

Jacquelyn L Slaton

Jacqueline Lopardo

April Carr

Colleen Scroll

Antonette Parker

Barbie Conner

Nakia Melecio

Ameer Muhammad

Lydia Cole

Shelby Swan

Phillip Olaleye

Nikita Howard

Jennifer Abdullah

Nancy Hale

Julian Allen

Eric Koester

Leroy Basnight

Kira Howard

Constance Kiser

Laurence Wingo

Charnae Knight

Delovely Boyd

Kathleen Anne Dolan

Cassie Wilcox

Melody Taylor

Vikki Stokes

Anna Walton

Nurah Petross

Arla davenport

Asha Hagood

Natosha Scott

Sandy Welfare

Tazar Gissentanner

Brooke Bosley

Shirley Wallace

Floyd Glinsey Sr.

Marcus Alleyne

Raja Schaar

Chad Edmonds

Naimah Abdullah

Victor Montgomery

Iman Ellis Bowen

James Gilmartin

Desiree Rivers

Shaun Martin

Ladena Ingram

Robbin Boyd

Marcus Alleyne

Lori Lypson

Andrea Jenkins

Ruqayya Muhammad

Bernard Wallace

Tamera Anderson-Hunt

Latrice McBee Johnson

Tamika Adams

Bryan Houser

Elizabeth Campbell

Okolo Rashid

Appendix

———

AUTHOR'S NOTE

Abdulrahim, Raja. "Nation of Islam Member Peddles Bean Pies a Ritual Going Back Decades." *Seattle Times,* June 19, 2011. https://www.seattletimes.com/life/food-drink/nation-of-is-lam-member-peddles-bean-pies-a-ritual-going-back-decades/>

Davies, Emily. "70 Years Ago, Henrietta Lacks's Cells Were Taken Without Consent. Now, Her Family Wants Justice." *The Washington Post*, October 4, 2021. https://www.washingtonpost.com/local/legal-issues/henrietta-lacks-family-sues-compa-ny/2021/10/04/810ffa6c-2531-11ec-8831-a31e7b3de188_story.html

Eligon, John, Audra Burch, Dionne Searcey, and Richard Oppel Jr. "Black Americans Face Alarming Rates of Coronavirus Infection in Some States." *New York Times*, April 4, 2020. https://www.nytimes.com/2020/04/07/us/coronavirus-race.html

"Muhammad Speaks." *Muhammad Speaks,* October 29, 1971. https://jstor.org/stable/10.2307/community.28592125.

Taylor, Ula Yvette. *The Promise of Patriarchy*. Chapel Hill: University of North Carolina Press, 2017.

US Census Bureau. "Year: 1900; Census Place: Pierce Chapel, Lee, Alabama;" Page: 1; Enumeration District: 0040; FHL microfilm: 1240025.

US Census Bureau. "Year: *1910*; Census Place: *Grahams Store, Lee, Alabama*;" Roll: *T624_22*; Page: *8B*; Enumeration District: *0170*; FHL microfilm: *1374035*.

CHAPTER 1

AJC Staff. "Hundreds More Were Lynched in The South Than Previously Known: Report." *Atlanta Journal Constitution*, June 14, 2017. https://www.ajc.com/news/local/hundreds-more-were-lynched-the-south-than-previously-known-report/gOEGts-Sud4utD6Uiqkx1LN/.

Brown, Ashley and Olivia Nichols. "Racial Terror in Lee County." Accessed January 14, 2021. https://www.leecountyremembrance.org/research

Huffman, Keith. "Program on Creek Indian Removal from Alabama to Be Featured Saturday at Museum of East Alabama." *Opelika-Auburn News*, April 19, 2018. https://oanow.com/news/local/program-on-creek-indian-removal-from-alabama-to-be-featured-saturday-at-museum-of-east/article_5fb39b36-5a97-5701-93e0-c791bf7ad769.html.

Robertson, Campbell. "Memorial in Alabama Will Honor Victims of Lynching." *New York Times*, August 15, 2016. https://www.

nytimes.com/2016/08/16/us/memorial-alabama-victims-lynching.html

Smith, Dorothy. "Life in the Black Community of Montgomery, Alabama from 1900 to 1910, as Reflected in the Montgomery Daily Advertiser and Other Related Sources." 1975. Accessed September 3, 2021, https://radar.auctr.edu/islandora/object/cau.td%3A1975_smith_dorothy_a

Visualizing the Red Summer. "Timeline." Accessed June 22, 2021. https://visualizingtheredsummer.com/

CHAPTER 2

Bates, Beth Tompkins. "Chapter 4: Drawing the Color Line in House, 19151935." *Making of Black Detroit in the Age of Henry Ford*, Chapel Hill: University of North Carolina Press, 2012.

Bates, Beth Tompkins. "Making Of Black Detroit in The Age of Henry Ford." Chapel Hill: University of North Carolina Press, 2014.

FBI Records. Report on The Nation of Islam. August 15, 1942. https://vault.fbi.gov/Nation%20of%20Islam

Muhammad, Zakiyyah. *Mother of the Nation: Clara Evans Muhammad, Volume 1: The Formative Years: 1899–1930.* Self-published, 2020.

Muhammad, Elijah. *The True History of Master Fard Muhammad.* Atlanta: MEMPS Publications, 2014.

Lincoln, Eric. *The Black Muslims in America*. Queens, New York: Kayode Publications Ltd., 1973.

CHAPTER 3

Ellis, Jackie, Chris Dowrick, and Mari Lloyd-Williams. "The Long-Term Impact of Early Parental Death: Lessons from a Narrative Study." *Journal of the Royal Society of Medicine*. 106, (2013): 57–67.

Haine, Rachel, Sharlene Wolchik, Irwin Sandler, Roger Millsap, and Tim Ayers. "Positive Parenting as a Protective Resource for Parentally Bereaved Children." *Death Studies*. 30, (2006): 1–28.

Rostila, Mikael and Jan Saarela." Time Does Not Heal All Wounds: Mortality Following the Death of a Parent." *Journal of Marriage and Family*. 73, (2011): 236–249.

CHAPTER 4

US Commission on Civil Rights. Statement on Affirmative Action. Washington, DC, 1977. https://eric.ed.gov/?id=ED146310

CHAPTER 8

Hurston, Zora Neale. *Their Eyes Were Watching God*. London: Virago, 1986.

Renzulli, Linda and Lorraine Evans. "School Choice, Charter Schools, and White Flight." *Social Problems* (2005): 398–418. https://doi.org/10.1525/sp.2005.52.3.398

Made in the USA
Monee, IL
17 May 2022

96600626R00190